COOKING FOR COCO

COOKING
FOR COCO

Naturally delicious baby food recipes from a chef's kitchen

Siân Blunos

CARROLL & BROWN PUBLISHERS LIMITED

Dedicated to William Gilbert Williams 1928–2002
MA, MB, M.Chir, FRCS   Cardio Thoracic Surgeon

I am dedicating this book to my dad who died just four days before Coco's first birthday. She was his only granddaughter and he desperately wanted to see her grow
up, but it wasn't to be … I miss him so much. He once said to me "She is a gift," and so she is.

To Mum, who has been incredibly strong and dignified – I can only admire her courage. She and Dad were soulmates.

To Martin – this year we have had more to deal with than most couples have to cope with in a lifetime. We are built of strong stuff and will get through it.
You are my soulmate … I love you.

To my two brothers, Huw and Richard, whom I simply adore – I am so lucky to have such a close family.

To Leon and Max, my boys, who have tried nearly all the recipes in this book – I think the world of them, and of course, my little Coco who inspired me to write.

To Omi and Poppi, Martin's parents – for all their love and support over the years.

First published in 2003 in the United Kingdom by

Carroll & Brown Publishers Limited
20 Lonsdale Road
London NW6 6RD

Managing Art Editor Emily Cook
Project Editor Carla Masson
Photographers Andrew Davis, Jules Selmes

Text © Siân Blunos 2003
Illustrations and compilation © Carroll & Brown Limited 2003

A CIP catalogue record for this book is available from the British Library.

ISBN 1-903258-70-7

10 8 6 4 2 1 3 5 7 9

Reproduced by Colourscan Singapore. Printed and bound in Singapore by Tien Wah Press.

contents

foreword

When my husband Martin and I first met I was employed as his second chef. We didn't get on well at all – he didn't like women in the kitchen, but I soon changed that! We were married in 1989. Leon was born later that year, Max followed in 1991 and then Coco came along in 2001.

I have cooked home-made food for all my children, and when Coco arrived I resolved to collect together all my tried-and-tested recipes and share with other mums just how easy it can be to make your own delicious dishes and batch cook them so that they are always available in your freezer.

All parents want to give their children the best start in life and, obviously, food plays a big part in this. It's essential that children have a good, balanced diet and that the food you give them is packed with the proteins, vitamins and minerals they need for healthy growth and mental development. What children eat from early on can also set the pattern for their future eating habits, and introducing them to a wide range of flavours, colours and textures will make them less likely to become fussy eaters later. I also believe that the food served to children should *look* like food – not teddy bears or dinosaurs, but attractive in itself, colourful and tempting. Gimmicky foods take away the primary pleasures of taste, colour and texture, and you may find that your child feels more strongly about the animal shape than the food itself.

When you prepare food for your children using fresh ingredients you know you are giving them the best. It's a complete myth that children are by nature difficult to please – they certainly won't eat certain foods if they are not offered them in the first place! Some mums are scared to have a go at home cooking for babies and children. Don't be: there is nothing nicer than seeing the delight on your baby's face as he or she tucks into a new taste sensation. One of Coco's first words to me was "Mmmore!"

introduction

weaning your baby

Most babies are ready to begin the weaning process by around four to six months old, but it is always advisable to check with your health visitor before you begin. When beginning to wean, start feeding with baby rice, fruit and vegetable purées. With Coco and the boys I introduced one flavour at a time, so if anything did upset them, I knew exactly what it was. When I was sure which foods they could tolerate, I started combining flavours.

Babies are born with a store of iron that lasts for about six months. So around that time it is important to introduce iron-rich foods – such as red meats, liver and pulses, as well as dried fruit – into their diets.

The *Ready, Steady, Start!* and *Missy Independent* chapters give simple recipes for when you first start weaning your baby and for when your little one is old enough to begin to feed her- or himself. Apart from these two chapters I have not divided the recipes into age groups – they are all delicious and useful for all members of the family.

It may help you to know that babies' appetites differ. To begin with, some will eat only a few spoonfuls; others start with big appetites – mine all did. With that in mind the recipes are geared to produce roughly six to eight portions.

If your baby does not like something immediately, leave it for a while, then re-introduce it at a later date. I have spoken to health visitors and nutritionists who say that a lot of mums tend not to re-introduce a flavour or food after their baby has rejected it for the first time. Babies' taste buds develop, so leave it for a few weeks and then try it again – you may be surprised!

salt and sugar

It is recommended that you do not add salt to your baby's food for at least the first year, as a baby's kidneys are not yet developed enough to cope with it. Even after a year salt should be kept to a minimum. Now that Coco is nearly two, I do season some of the dishes very slightly to bring out the flavours – but this is optional.

Many of the recipes in this book require unsalted stock. Most shop-bought stock cubes contain artificial additives, flavour enhancers and colours. They are also extremely high in salt – some cubes contain as much as 18g per 100ml of stock. Look out for low-salt stock (in the form of cubes or concentrated pastes) available from health food shops and some supermarkets. (The good ones contain about 0.03g salt per 100ml of stock). You can also make your own stock and freeze it in batches. You will find recipes for all the basic stocks in *Basic Recipes* at the back of the book.

The same could be said of sugar: don't use too much – it will most probably encourage a sweet tooth and may lead to gum and tooth problems. Not adding sugar to their food helps babies and toddlers to appreciate natural tastes. Most fruits and vegetables are naturally sweet anyway and, though they may taste bland to you, they are sweet enough to a baby's sensitive palate.

fresh ingredients

Buy the best ingredients and produce you can afford for your baby. Most of us would prefer to buy only organic produce – grown without the routine use of pesticides, fungicides and chemicals, and free from artificial additives, sweeteners, flavourings and colourings – but it can be expensive and a wide range may not always be available. Look out for locally produced fruit and vegetables – because they haven't travelled far, they are fresher and retain more nutrients. The main thing is to make sure you are using plenty of fresh fruit and vegetables in your baby's diet.

family fare

As your baby gets older you will be using more adult foods for meals and snacks. After all, why should there be special children's meals? In my grandparents' day there wasn't such a thing! Start your children eating a wide range of foods when they are young – they shouldn't need a different menu.

Most of the recipes in this book are suitable for the whole family. For the other family members you just have to add seasoning to taste and, of course, you won't have to process any of the ingredients, although the vegetable purées make lovely accompaniments to meat and fish.

Eating as a family is important. I know it is not always possible with the busy lives we lead, but do try and make an effort. It is vital for children to know how to behave at the table and to learn etiquette as part of growing up. I also think it is important to be able to take your children to a restaurant. (We don't seem to do this much in Britain, but on the Continent it is a way of life.) You cannot expect children to behave properly in a restaurant if they never eat at the table with the family.

The great thing about cooking in batches is that if you go out for lunch, you can take a portion of frozen food with you and ask the restaurant to reheat it – no one has ever said no to me. The same goes for when you're invited by friends.

recipe measurements

Please note that all the measurement conversions are approximate. Because some of them have been rounded up or down, it is important not to mix the imperial and metric measurements when following a recipe – stay with either one or the other.

blending

Electric hand-held blenders are very easy to use for purées and sauces, but not for larger quantities. I would not be without my food processor. You need a good, strong and robust brand because you'll be using it a lot!

You will need to experiment to get the proper proportion of liquid to solid to make the food a consistency that your baby is happy with. Until your baby is about seven months old, foods with skins or seeds will have to be strained after puréeing. To do this, push the food through a mesh strainer using a spoon or a rubber spatula.

When I refer to correcting the texture in the recipes, I mean achieving a texture that your baby is able to manage. Start with a smooth consistency, then gradually introduce more chewy food as your baby's eating skills develop, from around seven to nine months. Studies have shown that the late introduction of chewy foods can be associated with an increased likelihood of a toddler being choosy about food.

Potatoes are used in many recipes in this book, so it is worth noting that they are not really suitable for blending or processing as they become gluey. I usually simply mash them and then mix with a purée.

freezing food

The recipes are designed for freezing, unless stated otherwise. Always label and date the portioned dishes before freezing so you can use the older ones first. You can keep the food frozen for about three months.

Before serving or freezing, divide the food into equal portions – you will be the best judge of the amount your baby eats. Let the food cool completely before you freeze it.

Some people use ice-cube trays or small plastic containers to freeze their baby's food. You can use them for the basic purées, but I prefer to use freezer cling film or food wrap for storing

food portions, as it doesn't take up too much space. Simply lay a piece of cling film on the table, spoon a portion of the food into the middle and wrap it up like a parcel (or use ties), then label and date. Lay the parcels flat on a tray and freeze them. Once they are frozen, you can store them one on top of the other.

reheating

It is extremely important to reheat dishes properly. Bacteria breed profusely in warm conditions, so make sure the food is piping hot throughout. Reheat the food directly from frozen. Remove the cling film, and either reheat in a saucepan on the stove, or in a microwave. Once the food is piping hot, stir well to remove any hot spots and allow it to cool until it is the right temperature for your baby to eat. If, by any chance, you have anything left uneaten, discard it immediately – do not reheat, refreeze or re-use under any circumstances.

hygiene

Obviously cleanliness is of the utmost importance when looking after babies, especially when it comes to preparing, storing and reheating their food. The following points may seem obvious, but they are worth noting anyway.

Always wash your own and your baby's hands before touching food. In your baby's first six to seven months, sterilise all the utensils you use to feed her or him. After that time, your baby is usually crawling, exploring everything and putting anything that fits into her or his mouth, so sterilisation becomes a little pointless. However, you should continue to ensure that all equipment is thoroughly clean and that work surfaces are wiped over with an appropriate anti-bacterial cleaner.

Commercial kitchens use colour-coded chopping boards to help to avoid cross-contamination: different colours are used for raw and cooked fish, meats and vegetables. At home, I recommend that you have at least two chopping boards: one for raw and the other for cooked foods, always remembering to clean them thoroughly after use, and never mixing them up. This also applies to the knives you use.

Lastly, wash your kitchen cloths and tea towels daily to avoid the build-up of bacteria.

ready, steady, start!

Weaning your baby onto solid foods is an exciting time of new tastes, textures and colours, and it's wonderful to see your little one enjoying "real" food!

Remember, try one flavour at a time at first and don't be afraid to "experiment" – your baby will love some tastes and loathe others, but do try them again after a couple of weeks. Soon you'll begin to combine flavours that your baby likes, and you'll really see those taste buds starting to develop.

This chapter has some simple purées to try after you have tested out single flavours and your baby is happy with them. All the other recipes in the book are suitable for babies from six months onwards, unless stated otherwise.

pear purée

apple purée

Pears are very easy to digest, making them ideal for starting to wean your baby. Try Williams or Comice for this recipe.

Makes: 6–8 portions

6 ripe dessert pears, peeled
Juice of ½ lemon
Sugar to taste

1 Quarter the pears and use a teaspoon to scoop out the core. Put the quarters into a saucepan and cover with water. Add the lemon juice and a little sugar.

2 Bring to simmering point and gently poach the pears for about 5 minutes or until the fruit is soft – the time will depend on the ripeness of the fruit.

3 Leave to cool in the syrup, then purée in a food processor or with a hand-held blender. Divide into portions and serve or freeze.

For this dish I prefer to use Cox's Orange Pippins as I think their flavour is excellent. But any dessert apple will do.

Makes: 6–8 portions

10oz/275g peeled and cored apple
Juice of ½ lemon

1 Cut the apples into small pieces and place in a non-reactive saucepan with the lemon juice. Seal with a tight-fitting lid. Place on the stove, bring to a simmer and cook slowly, stirring from time to time, for 8 to 10 minutes or until soft.

2 When done, remove the pan from the heat and purée in a food processor or with a hand-held blender. Leave to cool, then divide into portions and serve or freeze.

preparation tip

There is no need to add water to the pan because the slow cooking will draw out the natural juices within the apples, which will turn to steam and soften the fruit – hence the need for a tight-fitting lid on the pan.

nectarine or peach purée

The nectarine is a smooth-skinned member of the peach family. Make sure the ones you use are ripe – in other words sweet and juicy. The best time to make this is in summer when there is an abundance of fruit in the shops.

Makes: 6–8 portions

4 ripe nectarines or peaches
1½ tablespoons/22g sugar

1 Place the whole fruit in a pan with the sugar. Cover with water and bring to simmering point. Simmer for about 10 minutes or until the fruit is soft.

2 Strain off the syrup and set the nectarines or peaches aside to cool. Peel, skin and stone. Whiz the fruit flesh in a food processor, or use a hand-held blender. Divide into portions, then serve or freeze.

banana and apple purée

This is an ideal combination. You can mix the purée with yoghurt or use it in a crumble (see page 74). The reason why you need to cook the banana is to prevent it from going black when it is frozen.

Makes: 6–8 portions

6oz/175g peeled bananas
Juice of ½ lemon
1 dessertspoon/10g caster sugar
6oz/175g apple purée (see page 13)

1 Slice the bananas and place them in a saucepan with the lemon juice and sugar. Cover with a tight-fitting lid and cook over gentle heat for about 5 minutes or until soft, depending on the ripeness.

2 Mash and leave to cool. Blend with the apple purée and divide into portions, then serve or freeze.

tropical fruit purée

Be adventurous and give your baby a taste of tropical fruit. This is a very quick recipe as there is no cooking involved. Use really ripe fruit to ensure the best flavour and the best nutritional value.

Makes: 6–8 portions

1 mango
1 paw-paw (or papaya)
2 bananas
1 kiwi fruit
2 tablespoons/30ml coconut milk

1 Peel all the fruit. Cut the paw-paw in half and scoop out the seeds. Cut the fruit into small pieces.

2 Place all the ingredients into a food processor, or use a hand-held blender, whiz and then pass through a sieve to remove the kiwi seeds. Divide the purée into portions, then serve or freeze.

nutritional info

Mango is rich in beta-carotene, with small amounts of B vitamins, vitamin C and some minerals, such as calcium and magnesium, which strengthen bones and teeth and promote healthy muscles.

Paw-paw is rich in beta-carotene, vitamin C, calcium and magnesium.

Banana is rich in beta-carotene, folic acid and B vitamins, calcium and other minerals, as well as slow-releasing sugars.

Kiwi fruit is rich in beta-carotene, vitamin C and potassium. It is also high in fibre.

aubergine purée

This purée has a fantastic smooth flavour and is lovely on its own. I also use it in my Lamb and Aubergine Bake (see page 65).

Makes: 6–8 portions

2 tablespoons/30ml olive oil
1 clove garlic, peeled and crushed
2–3 medium aubergines (about 2lb/900g), peeled and finely diced
½ pint/275ml unsalted chicken stock (see page 125)
2 sprigs thyme

1 Heat the oil in a saucepan. Gently fry the garlic and aubergine for about 5 minutes. Add the stock and thyme, and bring to the boil. Reduce the heat and simmer, covered, for 5 minutes. Remove the lid and simmer for a further 20 to 25 minutes or until the liquid has been absorbed.

2 Remove the thyme sprigs, leave to cool and blend. Divide into portions, then serve or freeze.

carrot and turnip purée

Babies love the sweetness of this vegetable purée.

Makes: 6–8 portions

3 medium carrots (about 14oz/400g), peeled and diced
1 medium turnip (about 6oz/175g), peeled and sliced

1 Put the carrots and turnip in a saucepan, cover with cold water and bring to the boil. Cover, reduce the heat and simmer for 10 to 15 minutes or until tender.

2 Strain the vegetables and let cool. Purée and divide into portions, then serve or freeze.

broccoli, carrot, leek and potato cheese

Using cheese in this recipe is a good way to start introducing dairy products to your baby's diet.

Makes: 6–8 portions

3 medium potatoes (about 12oz/350g), for mash
½ pint/275ml white sauce (see page 121)
1 medium carrot (about 6oz/175g), peeled and diced
1 medium leek (about 4oz/100g), finely diced
2 heads broccoli (about 1lb/450g), cut into florets
2oz/50g hard cheese such as Cheddar, grated

1 Prepare the potato mash (see page 121) and the white sauce and set aside.

2 Cook the vegetables until tender for the following approximate cooking times: carrot 12 minutes; leek 6 minutes; broccoli 5 minutes. Drain.

3 Add the grated cheese to the hot white sauce and whisk until the cheese has melted. In a food processor whiz the vegetables together, adding the cheese sauce a little at a time. Mix with the mashed potato, adding the rest of the sauce, if necessary, to correct the texture. Divide into portions, then serve or freeze.

fennel and potato cheese

Cooked fennel has a delicate aniseed flavour. It aids digestion so may also help to prevent or soothe colic in babies.

Makes: 6–8 portions

2–3 medium potatoes (about 10oz/275g), for mash
¼ pint/150ml white sauce (see page 121)
1 small bulb fennel, trimmed
2oz/50g hard cheese, grated
1 tablespoon chopped parsley

1 Prepare the potato mash (see page 121) and the white sauce and set aside.

2 To a saucepan of boiling water, add the fennel and cook for about 8 minutes or until tender. Drain.

3 Add the grated cheese and parsley to the hot white sauce, whisking until the cheese has melted. Whiz the fennel in a food processor, adding the white sauce a little at a time. (For older children you can cut the fennel into small pieces instead of puréeing it.) Add the sauce mixture to the mashed potato. Divide into portions, then serve or freeze.

parsnip, lentil and sweet potato purée

Both parsnips and sweet potatoes have a delicious sweet taste that babies love, especially when they are first trying puréed foods.

Cut the sweet potato into smaller pieces than the parsnip as the sweet potato takes longer to cook.

nutritional info

Parsnip is a good source of starch and fibre. It is rich in folic acid, vitamin C and small amounts of the B vitamins. It is also rich in calcium, magnesium and potassium.

Lentils are a very nutritious source of protein and cholesterol as well as fibre, which helps to regulate blood sugar levels. It is also full of iron, magnesium, potassium and the B vitamins.

Sweet potatoes are much richer in vitamins, minerals and antioxidants than normal potatoes and are very high in vitamins C and E, as well as iron and potassium.

Makes: 6–8 portions

1oz/25g unsalted butter
1 tablespoon/30ml olive oil
1 small onion, peeled and chopped
1 small clove garlic, peeled and chopped
2 sweet potatoes (about 15oz/425g), peeled and finely diced
1 large parsnip (about 10oz/275g), peeled and diced
4oz/100g red lentils, washed in cold water and drained
1½oz/40g tomato purée
About ½ pint/275–300ml water or unsalted vegetable stock (see page 125)

1 Melt the butter and oil in a saucepan and gently fry the onion and garlic for about 2 minutes. Stir in the sweet potatoes, parsnip, lentils and tomato purée, and fry for a further 2 minutes.

2 Pour enough water or stock into the pan to cover the vegetables and bring to the boil. Cook for about 25 minutes, stirring occasionally and adding more water or stock if necessary. Strain the vegetables over a bowl and reserve the cooking liquid.

3 Whiz the vegetable mixture in a food processor, adding the reserved liquid to correct the texture if necessary. Cool and divide into portions, then serve or freeze.

simple root vegetables

Swede is an extremely good vegetable for weaning, as it has a sweet taste that most babies like. Swede is also a great source of energy since it contains natural sugars and starches.

Makes: 6–8 portions

4 medium potatoes
  (about 1lb/450g), for mash
1oz/25g unsalted butter
½ swede (about 6oz/175g),
  peeled and finely diced
1 medium parsnip (about 6oz/175g),
  peeled, cored and finely diced
1 medium carrot (about 6oz/175g),
  peeled and finely diced
¾ pint/425ml unsalted vegetable stock
  (see page 125)

1 Prepare the potato mash (see page 121) and set aside.

2 In a saucepan, melt the butter. Add the swede, parsnip and carrot and gently fry for about 5 minutes. Cover with the vegetable stock, bring to the boil and simmer for about 20 minutes until tender, stirring occasionally. Strain over a bowl and reserve the cooking liquid.

3 Whiz the vegetables in a food processor. Add the mashed potato and enough of the reserved cooking liquid to obtain the appropriate texture. Cool and divide into portions, then serve or freeze.

serving tip

For a baby older than six months, it is not necessary to blend the vegetables in a food processor. Simply mash all the vegetables and potatoes together, adding some of the reserved cooking liquid to achieve the desired texture.

butternut squash or pumpkin mash

This dish is very simple and yummy! It is an ideal weaning food as it is easy to digest. Butternut squash and pumpkins have a firm texture, are slightly sweet and the flesh has a lovely golden colour.

Makes: 6–8 portions

1 butternut squash or pumpkin (about 12oz/350g)
Knob of unsalted butter or a little of baby's usual milk

1 Peel and halve the squash or pumpkin. Use a spoon to scoop out the seeds and dice into 1in/2.5cm pieces.

2 Put into a saucepan of boiling water and bring back to the boil. Reduce the heat and simmer gently for 8 to 10 minutes or until soft. Remove from the heat and drain well.

3 Mash the butternut squash or pumpkin, adding the butter or milk to taste. Leave to cool and divide into portions, then serve or freeze.

more about...
pumpkin

Squash and pumpkin are very versatile and can be used for sweet dishes such as pies or for savoury dishes such as soups. They can also be mashed, creamed, roasted or baked.

celeriac and potato mash

Celeriac gives mashed potato a lovely flavour and Coco adores it. Make sure that you dice the celeriac and potatoes evenly so that they will be cooked through at the same time.

Makes: 6–8 portions

3 medium potatoes (about 12oz/350g), peeled and diced
1 medium celeriac (about 12oz/350g), peeled and diced
Knob of unsalted butter or a little of baby's usual milk

1 Put the potato and celeriac into a saucepan and cover with cold water. Bring to the boil, cover and reduce the heat. Cook for about 20 minutes or until tender.

2 Strain, then purée in a food processor, adding the butter or milk. Cool and divide into portions, then serve or freeze.

marrow purée

Marrow is a little bland, but with the addition of some herbs and spices, as well as butter, it is a nice early purée for baby to try.

Makes: 6–8 portions

10oz/275g marrow, peeled
1oz/25g unsalted butter
1 small onion, peeled and chopped
Pinch of mace
1 sprig thyme

1 Halve the marrow and use a spoon to scoop out the seeds in the middle. Cut the flesh into ½in/1cm cubes.

2 Melt the butter in a saucepan, add the onion and gently fry it for about 4 minutes or until soft. Add the marrow, mace and thyme, cover and cook gently for 15 to 20 minutes or until soft.

3 Mash or purée and leave to cool. Divide into portions, then serve or freeze.

beetroot purée

Coco loves this purée because of the bright colour and sweetness of the beetroot. For a change, you can also mix it with equal parts of apple purée, adding just a dash of lemon juice.

Makes: 6–8 portions

1lb/450g beetroot, peeled

1 Cut the beetroot into evenly sized pieces. Put them in a saucepan and cover with cold water. Bring to the boil, reduce the heat and simmer, covered, for about 40 minutes or until tender.

2 Strain, cool and purée. Divide into portions, then serve or freeze.

butterbean purée

As with all pulses, serve this dish only occasionally, because too much might give your baby wind. If you're in a hurry, you can use strained tinned butterbeans instead of dried.

Makes: 6–8 portions

6oz/175g dried butterbeans, soaked overnight
1 small clove garlic, peeled and crushed
Squeeze of lemon juice

1 Rinse the butterbeans and put them in a saucepan. Cover with cold water, add the garlic and bring to the boil. Cover, reduce the heat and cook for about 75 minutes, topping up with water as required. When the butterbeans are soft, drain and cool.

2 Simply put the cooked butterbeans and garlic into a food processor and whiz. Add a squeeze of fresh lemon juice. Cool and divide into portions, then serve or freeze.

nutritional info

Butterbeans, also known as Lima beans, contain iron, are high in protein and fibre and low in fat. They also contain some B vitamins.

Garlic is renowned for its health-giving benefits. It can lower the risk of heart disease, helping to reduce cholesterol and to improve circulation. It is rich in folic acid, vitamin C, calcium, iron and magnesium, and contains small amounts of B vitamins.

serving tip

Coco finds butterbean purée bland without seasoning, which is why I add garlic and lemon juice to this dish. This purée also works well served with meat dishes as a change from potato. Martin serves it with slow-braised belly of pork in the restaurant – I love it. It has a fantastic thick texture.

everyday coco

The following recipes are, as the title says, dishes that I cook on a daily basis for the whole family, but also particular favourites of Coco's. They are generally less complicated and time-consuming than some of the recipes in the Gourmet Coco *chapter, but they're just as tasty.*

It is important to me that my children know what home-cooked food tastes like. Using fresh ingredients gives me peace of mind, because I know that each meal will be packed full of protein, vitamins and minerals. I also know that my children will have enough "fuel" to keep them going through their day.

Beware of buying ready-made meals and junk food. They are high in hidden fat, sugar and salt, and can lead to childhood obesity and behavioural problems.

cauliflower, leek and potato cheese

This is a very simple dish – one of Coco's favourites and, because it is so easy, one of mine too.

Makes: 6–8 portions

4 medium potatoes (about 1lb/450g), for mash

1 cauliflower (about 1lb/450g), cut into florets

2 medium leeks (about 6oz/175g), roughly chopped

½ pint/275ml white sauce (see page 121)

2oz/50g hard cheese, grated

1 Prepare the potato mash (see page 121) and set aside.

2 Put the cauliflower in a saucepan with rapidly boiling water. Cook, uncovered, for about 15 minutes or until tender.

3 In another saucepan, cover the leeks with a little water, bring to the boil and reduce the heat. Simmer for about 6 minutes until tender.

4 Make a cheese sauce by preparing the white sauce and whisking in the cheese until it has melted. Remove from the heat.

5 In a food processor, whiz the leeks and cauliflower together, adding the cheese sauce a little at a time. Add this mixture to the mashed potatoes, with more sauce, if required, to reach the correct texture. Leave to cool, then divide into portions and serve or freeze.

preparation tip

When cleaning the leeks, slit them lengthwise, keeping the root end intact. Separate the leaves and rinse them under running water to remove the sand or dirt that is often found between the layers.

courgette, onion and chestnut mushroom mash

I sometimes make these into little croquettes for the boys and Coco. Simply roll out the mixture into a large sausage on a floured table and cut it into 2in/5cm pieces. Dip the croquettes into beaten egg and cover in dried breadcrumbs (see page 123), then deep-fry them in oil.

Makes: 6–8 portions

3 medium potatoes (about 12oz/350g), for mash
1oz/25g unsalted butter
1 dessertspoon/10ml sunflower oil
1 small onion, peeled and finely chopped
1 clove garlic, peeled and crushed
2oz/50g chestnut mushrooms, finely diced
1 medium courgette (about 6oz/175g), quartered lengthwise and sliced
2oz/50g hard cheese, grated
A little of baby's usual milk

1 Prepare the potato mash (see page 121) and set aside.

2 Heat the butter and oil in a pan. Gently fry the onion, garlic, mushrooms, and courgette, cover and cook for about 10 minutes until tender. Sprinkle grated cheese over while the mixture is still warm so that it melts.

3 When cool, put the mixture into a food processor and whiz. Mix with the mashed potato, adding just enough milk to correct the texture. Divide into portions, then serve or freeze.

nutritional info

Courgettes are rich in beta-carotene, needed for a healthy skin and for protection against infection.

Mushrooms contain B vitamins, potassium, iron, protein and polysaccharides, which are known to stimulate the immune system.

tasty pasta with cheese, tomato and broccoli sauce

This dish introduces pasta to your baby's diet. Any pasta is fine for this recipe as it will be blended. As your baby gets older and is able to chew, you can use the small pasta shapes available in most supermarkets.

Makes: 6–8 portions

14oz/400g fresh tomato sauce (see page 122) or 1 x 14oz/400g tin chopped tomatoes
6oz/175g pasta (any shape)
1 small head broccoli (about 6oz/175g), cut into florets
1oz/25g unsalted butter
1 tablespoon/15ml olive oil
1 small onion, peeled and chopped
1 clove garlic, peeled and chopped
2oz/50g hard cheese, grated

1 Prepare the fresh tomato sauce and set aside.

2 Cook the pasta according to the package instructions, but do not add any salt. When cooked, rinse with water, then drain.

3 Put the broccoli in a saucepan of rapidly boiling water. Cook, uncovered, for about 5 minutes or until tender.

4 Melt the butter and oil in a pan, add the onion and garlic and fry gently, stirring occasionally, until soft. Add the tomato sauce or chopped tomatoes to the pan, bring to the boil, then reduce the heat and simmer for a few minutes to reduce and thicken the sauce. Add the cheese and stir until melted.

5 Whiz the pasta and broccoli in a food processor, adding the sauce a little at a time to reach the right consistency. Leave to cool, then divide into portions and serve or freeze.

27

veggie couscous

This dish is suitable after seven months. It can be served warm or cold as a salad. You can add some flaked cooked fish if you feel like a change.

Makes: 6–8 portions

9fl oz/250ml unsalted vegetable stock
  (see page 125)
4oz/100g couscous
2oz/50g frozen peas
2 large tomatoes, skinned, seeded
  and diced
2oz/50g tinned or frozen sweetcorn

1 Bring the stock to the boil, pour over the couscous and leave to stand until all the stock is absorbed (8 to 10 minutes).

2 Add the peas to a saucepan of rapidly boiling water. Cook, uncovered, for about 2 minutes. Drain and rinse in cold water.

3 Add the tomatoes, sweetcorn and peas to the couscous and mix. Leave to cool. Divide into portions and serve or freeze.

coco's favourite green vegetables with potatoes and cheese sauce

People think that children won't eat vegetables, but that has never been the case with my children – Coco just loves green veggies! Introduce vegetables early on, and you will help your child to develop a liking for them, while also giving him or her all the benefits of the vegetables' goodness.

Makes: 6–8 portions

1 large potato (about 6oz/175g), for
  mash
2oz/50g French beans
2oz/50g green beans
2oz/50g broccoli, cut into small florets
2oz/50g mange tout
2oz/50g frozen peas
½ pint/275ml white sauce (see page
  121)
2oz/50g hard cheese, grated

1 Prepare the potato mash (see page 121) and set aside.

2 Cook all the green vegetables in a saucepan of rapidly boiling water for the appropriate time, given in the table below. Drain and cut into manageable pieces.

3 Prepare the white sauce and whisk in the cheese until it is melted. Add the vegetables to the sauce, and mix with the mashed potato. Leave to cool, then divide into portions and serve or freeze.

Cooking times

French beans	5–6 minutes
Green beans	4–5 minutes
Broccoli	4–5 minutes
Mange tout	4–5 minutes
Peas (frozen)	2–3 minutes

vegetable and pearl barley broth

This is an ideal winter recipe. You can use any of the delicious winter root vegetables such as parsnip, swede, turnip, carrots or leeks. Mix and match to your baby's taste.

Makes: 6–8 portions

4oz/100g pearl barley
1oz/25g unsalted butter
1 tablespoon/15ml sunflower oil
2 medium leeks (about 6oz/175g), chopped
3oz/75g swede, peeled and chopped
3oz/75g turnips, peeled and chopped
1½oz/40g tomato purée
¾ pint/425ml water or unsalted vegetable stock (see page 125)
2oz/50g frozen peas

1 Wash the barley in cold water as it can be "gritty". Place in a saucepan, cover with cold water and bring to the boil. As soon as it reaches boiling point, remove from the heat and rinse in cold water before straining. This will get rid of some of the starch in the pearl barley.

2 Melt the butter and oil in a saucepan, add the leeks, swede and turnips and sweat for about 2 minutes.

3 Add the pearl barley and tomato purée and just enough water or stock to cover the vegetables in the pan. Bring to the boil and simmer, stirring occasionally, for about 50 minutes. Add more water or stock if required – the mixture needs to have quite a thick consistency.

4 Add the peas, cover the pan and continue to simmer until the pearl barley is very soft (about a further 5 minutes, but the older the pearl barley, the longer it takes to soften).

5 Strain the vegetable and pearl barley mixture over a bowl and reserve the liquid. Whiz the mixture in a food processor, adding more of the liquid to reach the correct texture. Alternatively, just mash the mixture for older babies. Leave to cool, then divide into portions and serve or freeze.

nutritional info

Pearl barley is highly nutritious and very easy to digest. It is rich in B vitamins and vitamin E, calcium and potassium, which is said to improve mental alertness.

Turnip is another great source of energy with its natural sugars and starches, and it also contains vitamin C.

quick pizza

You can use tuna instead of ham if you wish, or, for that matter, any other pizza topping your baby likes. The boys and Coco love pineapple on pizza – it goes well with ham. Simply cut two or three slices of tinned pineapple into chunks and sprinkle over with the ham and cheese. Alternatively, slice half a red pepper and a few button mushrooms to replace the ham for a vegetarian pizza.

If you want to bake the pizza right away instead of freezing it, do it at the same temperature as for the frozen pizza, but reduce the time to about 10 to 15 minutes.

Makes: 6–8 portions

1 quantity Basic Scone dough (see page 112)
6oz/175g fresh tomato sauce (see page 123), passata or tinned chopped tomatoes
4oz/100g hard cheese, grated
2oz/50g cooked ham, thinly sliced

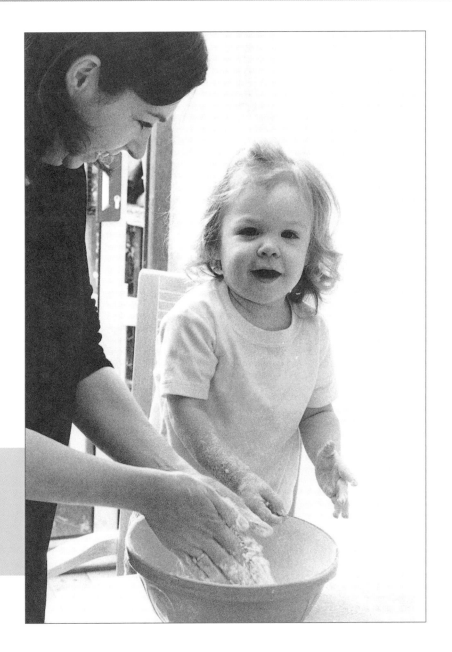

1 Roll the scone dough into an oblong shape about ⅛in/3mm thick and put onto a baking tray.

2 If you are using tinned tomatoes, whiz in a food-processor or with a hand-held blender. Cover the pizza base with a thin layer of tomato, then sprinkle with the cheese and the ham.

3 Put the pizza into the fridge to set for about 30 minutes. Then cut into 6 to 8 portions, leaving them on the tray. Freeze and, once frozen, wrap individually.

4 When needed, cook from frozen for about 20 minutes in an oven preheated to 200°C, 400°F.

home-made baked beans

Tinned baked beans are usually high in sugar, so give home-made baked beans a go. Once your child has eaten these a few times, he or she is certain to prefer your variety to any commercial brand!

Makes: 6–8 portions

6oz/175g dried haricot beans
14oz/400g fresh tomato sauce (see
    page 122) or 1 x 14oz/400g tin
    chopped tomatoes
1oz/25g unsalted butter
1 tablespoon/15ml olive oil
1 small onion, peeled and finely
    chopped
1 clove garlic, peeled and crushed
¾ pint/425ml unsalted chicken or
    vegetable stock (see page 125)
1 bay leaf
2 sprigs fresh thyme

1 Soak the beans in cold water overnight. Strain, cover with water again and simmer until tender (between 1¼–1½ hours).

2 Prepare the fresh tomato sauce and set aside.

3 Heat the butter and oil in a pan and gently fry the onion and garlic for 4 minutes. Stir in the tomato sauce (or chopped tomatoes), stock and beans, add the bay leaf and thyme and bring to the boil. Reduce the heat and simmer, covered, over a very low heat, for a further 10 minutes, stirring occasionally and adding more water if required.

4 Remove the bay leaf and thyme. Purée, or leave as it is for older babies. Leave to cool, then divide into portions and freeze.

sausage and baked beans

Make sure you buy good-quality sausages. They should be full of meat and not bread, fat and artificial flavourings. Some butchers make their own, or you could visit a specialist sausage shop. Try a variety of types, such as pork or beef.

Makes: 6–8 portions

8oz/225g sausages
Home-made baked beans (see left)

1 Preheat the oven to 160ºC, 325ºF.

2 In a pan, fry the sausages over medium heat for about 5 minutes until brown. Put the baked beans into an ovenproof dish, add the sausages and bake for about 20 minutes.

3 Let cool and cut the sausages into chunks. Blend, divide into portions and serve or freeze.

poached cod in a parsley and fennel butter sauce

This is an easy way to make fish a larger part of your baby's diet. White fish is one of the best sources of protein, and is easily digested. I use the loin of cod as it rarely has any bones and is nice and thick.

Makes: 6–8 portions

1 small fennel bulb (about 4oz/100g), trimmed and cut into 8 pieces
1 pint/570ml unsalted fish stock (see page 125)
8oz/225g cod loin, skinned and boned
1½oz/40g unsalted butter
1 tablespoon chopped parsley

1 Bring a saucepan of water to a rapid boil, add the fennel pieces and cook for 8 to 10 minutes, or until tender. Rinse in cold water and strain, and then dice into small pieces.

2 Pour the stock into a pan and bring to simmering point. Add the cod and simmer for 5 to 7 minutes, depending on the thickness of the fish. When cooked through, remove the fish and set aside.

3 Reduce the stock over high heat for about 4 minutes and strain. Put ¼ pint/150ml of the reduced stock into a saucepan. Whisk in 1½oz/40g butter until smooth and add the parsley and the fennel.

4 Flake the fish into the sauce, or, for younger babies, whiz the fish in a food processor then add to the sauce. Leave to cool, then divide into portions and serve or freeze.

preparation tip

Trim the fennel by taking off the green stalks and outer layers (which may be brown) and shaving off the base. Cut it into quarters and trim the core, but do not separate the layers.

33

tinned pilchards in tomato sauce with creamy mashed potato

This dish is easy and nutritious, and so simple to make, but is probably something that you might not think of yourself. You can add some vegetables if you like, but Coco seems to like it as it is.

You can replace the pilchards with tinned sardines. Use three small tins (4½oz/120g each), and add some fresh tomato sauce to taste – about 3 or 4 tablespoons/45–60ml (see page 122).

Do not use fresh sardines, because it's very difficult to remove all the tiny bones. The bones of tinned sardines and pilchards are well cooked and very soft, so can be eaten by babies.

Makes: 6–8 portions

3–4 medium potatoes (about 12–14oz/350–400g), for mash
1 x 15oz/425g tin pilchards in tomato sauce

1 Prepare the potato mash (see page 121) and set aside.

2 Remove the larger, visible bones from the pilchards. There's no need to remove all the bones – they are very soft, as they have been cooked. Whiz the pilchards in a food processor or mash with a fork and simply add to the mashed potato.

3 Leave to cool, then divide into portions and serve or freeze.

"Oooh!"

nutritional info

Pilchards are rich in calcium and very high in omega-3 fatty acids.

Potatoes are a good source of carbohydrates, rich in folic acid and vitamin C and contain small amounts of minerals and B vitamins.

tuna fish with potato, chives and sweetcorn

This is such a simple dish, especially if you are pushed for time and need to prepare something tasty quickly.

Coco loves it now, but the first time she had it, at about four or five months, she spat it out all over the floor, much to her two older brothers' delight – they thought it was hilarious! In turn, knowing that she got a great reaction, this became a good game – so poor Leon and Max were ordered out of the room until Coco had settled down. After this, I didn't give this dish to Coco for about five weeks, at which time I re-introduced it to her diet.

If your baby doesn't like something, he or she will soon let you know. I didn't make a fuss, just took it away and re-introduced it a few weeks later.

Makes: 6–8 portions

1 x 12oz/350g tin sweetcorn
2 x 6oz/185g tins tuna fish in either oil or brine
Small bunch chives, washed and chopped
4 medium potatoes (about 1lb/450g), peeled and diced, for mash
2oz/50g unsalted butter
A little of baby's usual milk

1 Drain the sweetcorn and tuna. Whiz them in a food processor with the chives.

2 Prepare the potato mash (see page 121), adding the butter when you are mashing.

3 Add the tuna mixture to the potato with just enough milk to correct the texture of the dish.

4 Leave to cool, then divide into portions and serve or freeze. It's as simple as that!

35

tuna bake

This is a lovely dish for the whole family to share, but you can also blend it for baby and divide it into portions for freezing. Before baking, you can sprinkle the top of this dish with cheese or breadcrumbs, or you can simply leave it as it is.

Makes: 6–8 portions

14oz/400g fresh tomato sauce (see
    page 122) or 1 x 14oz/400g tin
    chopped tomatoes
6oz/175g pasta (any shape)
1oz/25g unsalted butter
1 tablespoon/15ml sunflower oil
1 small onion, peeled and chopped
1 x 6oz/185g tin tuna fish

1 Prepare the fresh tomato sauce and set aside.

2 Preheat the oven to 150°C, 300°F. *Gas 2*

3 Cook the pasta according to the package instructions, but do not add any salt. When cooked, rinse with water, then drain.

4 Heat the butter and oil in a pan, and gently fry the onion for about 3 to 4 minutes until soft. Add the tomato sauce or chopped tomatoes and bring to simmering point. Then add the tuna.

5 Put the pasta into an ovenproof dish, pour over the tomato and tuna sauce, mix together and bake in the oven for about 20 minutes.

6 Leave to cool and then whiz in a food processor. Divide into portions and serve or freeze.

nutritional info

Tuna fish is rich in omega-3 fatty acids, which are good for brain function, and is also a good source of protein, as well as vitamin D and zinc.

turkey pilau

In this recipe I have used diced turkey leg – you can use fillet or escalopes, but it might be a little drier. Use long-grain rice for this recipe – its firm structure keeps the grains separate when cooked.

You can also use brown rice – it has a lovely nutty texture and is good to encourage your baby to chew. It takes slightly longer to cook, but it is more nutritious than white rice.

Makes: 6–8 portions

1oz/25g unsalted butter
4oz/100g turkey leg meat, cubed
1 small onion, peeled and chopped
6oz/175g long-grain rice
1¼ pint/725ml unsalted chicken stock
    (see page 125)

1 Preheat the oven to 160°C, 325°F.

2 Melt the butter in an ovenproof pan, and fry the turkey for 3 to 4 minutes, until brown. Add the onion and rice and cook for a further 3 to 4 minutes until the rice looks transparent, stirring all the time.

3 Add the stock, pouring it slowly, as it will bubble a lot at first. Cover with a tight-fitting lid and cook in the oven for 20 to 25 minutes until the stock is absorbed.

4 Leave to cool. Whiz in a food processor, adding more stock, if required, to reach the correct texture. Divide into portions and serve or freeze.

nutritional info

Turkey is packed with protein and is rich in selenium, which is an excellent antioxidant, as well as vitamin B_{12}.

chicken and pumpkin risotto

The pumpkin breaks down to make this a flavourful, moist dish, or butternut squash works just as well. Risotto rice, such as arborio or carnaroli, will give a far better result than normal long-grain rice.

Makes: 6–8 portions

1oz/25g unsalted butter
1 tablespoon/15ml olive oil
1 small onion, peeled and chopped
2 boneless chicken breasts (about
   10oz/275g), skinned and diced
1 small pumpkin or butternut squash
   (about 8oz/225g), peeled and diced
4oz/100g risotto rice
½ pint/275ml unsalted chicken stock
   (see page 125)

1 Heat the butter and oil in a pan and brown the onion and the chicken for about 2 minutes. Add the pumpkin (or butternut squash) and rice and fry for a further 1 minute.

2 Stir in the chicken stock and simmer for 20 to 25 minutes, stirring occasionally, until the rice is soft and the liquid has been absorbed. Leave to cool, then blend if required. Divide into portions and serve or freeze.

nutritional info

Chicken is a good source of lean protein.

Pumpkin and butternut squash are rich in beta-carotene, needed for healthy skin, for protection against infection and essential for night vision.

Rice provides essential carbohydrates.

pan-fried chicken livers with bacon and sage

Chicken livers are very nutritious and great for children. They are not as strong as other livers and go really well with sage.

Makes: 6–8 portions

2 slices (about 2oz/50g) lean
   unsmoked bacon, diced
3 medium potatoes (about 12oz/350g),
   for mash
8oz/225g chicken livers
1 tablespoon/15ml sunflower oil
1 small onion, peeled and chopped
¼ pint/150ml water, plus about
   2 tablespoons/30ml
4 fresh sage leaves, chopped

1 Soak the bacon in water for about 30 minutes to remove some of the salt.

2 Prepare the potato mash (see page 121) and set aside.

3 Clean the livers by rinsing lightly and drying them with kitchen paper. Remove the strings that connect the lobes and cut into small slices.

4 Heat the oil in a non-stick pan and fry the onion for 4 minutes, adding about 2 tablespoons water to finish cooking the onion, scraping the bottom of the pan with a wooden spoon.

5 When the water has evaporated, add the liver and bacon and fry for about 5 minutes. Add the sage and ¼ pint/150ml water. Simmer for a further 1 or 2 minutes until the liver is cooked.

6 Whiz the liver mixture in a food processor or leave it chunky for older children, and add to the mashed potato. Leave to cool, divide into portions and serve or freeze.

preparation tip

To remove the liver strings, hold down one lobe and pull the string out of it by pressing the other lobe with a knife blade. Holding down the string, repeat with the second lobe.

callum's stovies

One of Martin's chefs, Callum from Scotland, used to make this for the staff's lunch. Our own boys always had to have some – it is one of their favourites. Leon has even been known to eat it for breakfast. Coco was also introduced to this dish and – surprise, surprise! – she just loves it. This isn't really a good recipe to whiz in a food processor as the potatoes go gluey, so make it when your baby is old enough to chew the bacon pieces.

Makes: 6–8 portions

Knob of unsalted butter
1 small onion, peeled and sliced
4oz/100g lean bacon, cut into strips
4 large potatoes (about 1½lb/750g),
    peeled and thinly sliced
2 medium carrots (about 8oz/225g),
    peeled and thinly sliced
1 bay leaf
2 sprigs fresh thyme
Up to 1½ pints/850ml unsalted chicken
    stock (see page 125)

1 Heat the butter in a pan and gently fry the onion, bacon, potatoes and carrots for 3 to 4 minutes, stirring all the time. Add the bay leaf and thyme, cover and cook over medium heat without colouring for about 5 minutes, stirring occasionally. Pour in enough stock to cover and cook gently, covered, for about 45 minutes or until all the vegetables are tender.

2 Strain over a bowl, reserving the cooking liquid. Remove the herbs and mash the mixture together. Add some of the reserved stock to reach the correct texture.

3 Leave to cool, then divide into portions and serve or freeze.

nutritional info

Bacon is full of protein and a good source of vitamin B and zinc.

Onions help us to process fatty foods, helping to cut cholesterol.

Thyme is a herb known to aid digestion and has antiseptic properties.

41

pasta with red pepper, ham and broccoli in a creamy sauce

When Coco was about six months old, I tried to give her this dish and she didn't like it at all. If I put peppers into any of her meals she quickly showed her disapproval by spitting them out! But her taste changed – by the time she was eighteen months old, she ate slices of pepper raw.

Makes: 6 portions

6oz/175g pasta (any shape)
½ pint/275ml white sauce (see page 121)
1 small head broccoli (about 6oz/175g), cut into florets
1oz/25g butter
1 small onion, peeled and chopped
1 clove garlic, peeled and chopped
1 small red pepper, cored, seeded and chopped
4oz/100g good-quality sliced ham

1 Cook the pasta according to the package instructions, but do not add any salt. When cooked, rinse with water, then drain.

2 Prepare the white sauce and set aside.

3 Cook the broccoli in boiling water for about 5 minutes or until tender. Melt the butter in a pan and gently fry the onion, garlic and red pepper, stirring all the time. Cook for about 4 minutes. Add the white sauce and stir in the ham, pasta and broccoli.

4 For younger babies, whiz the mixture in a food processor, but leave chunky for older children. Leave to cool, then divide into portions and serve or freeze.

ham with lentils and carrot

If you do cook your own ham, this is a lovely way to use it and to use the stock, as long as it is not too salty. Otherwise, buy a good-quality ham from the supermarket or deli. Leon loves this fried as bubble and squeak for his breakfast!

Makes: 6–8 portions

4 medium potatoes (about 1lb/450g), for mash
1oz/25g unsalted butter
1 dessertspoon/10ml sunflower oil
1 small onion, peeled and chopped
1 small clove garlic, peeled and crushed
1 medium carrot (about 4oz/100g), peeled and finely diced
4oz/100g red lentils, washed
1 pint/570ml unsalted ham, chicken or vegetable stock (see page 125)
6oz/175g cooked ham, sliced or diced

1 Prepare the potato mash (see page 121) and set aside.

2 Heat the butter and oil in a pan and gently fry the onion, garlic, carrot and lentils for 4 minutes. Add enough stock to cover the vegetables and cook for 35 to 40 minutes, uncovered, stirring occasionally and adding a little more stock as it gets absorbed. Add the ham and cook for a further 3 to 4 minutes.

3 Remove the pan from the heat and leave to cool completely. Whiz the mixture in a food processor, then add to the mashed potato, adding more stock to correct the texture if necessary. For older babies you could mash the mixture or just leave it chunky. Divide into portions, then serve or freeze.

savoury lamb mince with marrow

Lamb is a good red-meat alternative to beef and an excellent source of iron and protein – both vital for growing children.

Marrow is quite bland on its own, but it goes really well with this dish and tastes delicious.

Makes: 6–8 portions

6oz/175g marrow, peeled
1oz/25g unsalted butter
1 tablespoon/15ml olive oil
1 small onion, peeled and chopped
1 clove garlic, peeled and crushed
8oz/225g lean lamb mince
1 dessertspoon/10ml tomato purée
1 bay leaf
½ pint/275ml unsalted lamb or chicken
   stock (see page 125)
6oz/175g cooked long-grain rice

"more...more...more!"

1 Halve the marrow and use a spoon to scoop out the middle. Cut the flesh into ½in/1cm cubes.

2 In a pan, heat the butter and oil and gently fry the onion and garlic for 3 to 4 minutes until soft. Add the lamb mince and fry for a further 4 minutes or until browned.

3 Add the marrow, tomato purée and the bay leaf. Stir in the stock, bring to the boil and reduce the heat. Simmer, covered, for about 15 minutes. Remove the lid and continue to cook for a further 15 minutes to let the sauce reduce and become syrupy. Remove the bay leaf. Then stir in the rice.

4 Purée in a food processor for babies, or leave chunky for older children. Leave to cool, then divide into portions and serve or freeze.

nain's "potatoes on top"

When Leon and Max were little and stayed with my mum and dad, Mum used to cook this for them. It became known as "Potatoes on Top" – the name has stuck ever since. They are both strapping lads now and still ask for Potatoes on Top when they go home.

Makes: 6–8 portions

4 medium potatoes (about 1lb/450g), scrubbed
1 tablespoon/15ml sunflower oil
1 small onion, peeled and chopped
1 clove garlic, peeled and crushed
12oz/350g lean minced beef
2 medium carrots (about 8oz/225g), peeled and diced
1 bay leaf
½ pint/275ml unsalted beef stock (see page 124)
2oz/50g hard cheese, grated

1 Put the potatoes, in their skins, in a saucepan, cover with cold water and bring to the boil. Cover, reduce the heat and cook for about 35 minutes, depending on size, until just tender. Pour off the water and leave to cool. When cold enough to handle, peel and slice into about ¼in/5mm slices. Set aside.

2 In a pan, heat the oil and gently fry the onion, garlic and mince until brown. Add the carrots and bay leaf and cover with stock. Cook for about 45 minutes, skimming off any fat.

3 Meanwhile, preheat the oven to 160ºC, 325ºF. Transfer the mince mixture to an ovenproof dish and layer the potato slices on top. Sprinkle the cheese over and bake for a further 45 minutes until the potatoes are crisp. Leave to cool, then divide into portions and serve or freeze.

preparation tip

This recipe is better not blended in a food processor because the potatoes become gluey. If your child is too small to eat the potato slices, mashed potato would be fine.

my grandmother's welsh lop scows

This recipe has been handed down through the generations to my grandmother and from her to me. Lop scows is particularly known in North Wales. There's nothing better than this stew on a cold winter's day – the children love it.

Makes: 8 generous portions

1lb/450g lean chuck steak, cut into
  cubes
1 onion, peeled and chopped
2 medium carrots (about 8oz/225g),
  peeled and diced large
½ swede (about 8oz/225g), peeled and
  diced large
4 medium potatoes (about 1lb/450g),
  peeled and diced large

1 Put the steak, onion, carrots and swede into a saucepan and just cover with water. Bring to the boil and skim the fat. Reduce the heat and simmer for about 1¼ hours, skimming now and again.

2 Add the potatoes, cover and cook for a further 20 minutes or until the potatoes are tender.

3 Cool and mash. (Do not blend the potatoes in a food processor.) Divide into portions, then serve or freeze.

ef and tomato casserole

This is a very wholesome dish, which can be enjoyed by the whole family. It contains lots of winter vegetables, full of goodness. Once you have browned all the ingredients, just put the casserole in the oven and forget about it for 1½ hours – it cooks itself.

Makes: 8 generous portions

14oz/400g fresh tomato sauce (see page 122) or 1 x 14oz/400g tin chopped tomatoes
2 tablespoons/30ml sunflower oil
8oz/225g lean chuck steak, diced
1 small onion, peeled and chopped
1 clove garlic, peeled and crushed
2oz/50g button mushrooms
½ swede (about 6oz/175g), peeled and finely diced
1 small leek (about 2oz/50g), chopped
1 small parsnip (about 4oz/100g), peeled and chopped
3 medium potatoes (about 12oz/350g), peeled and diced
1 pint/570ml unsalted beef stock (see page 124)
1 bay leaf

1 Prepare the fresh tomato sauce and set aside.

2 Preheat the oven to 160°C, 325°F.

3 Heat the oil in a heavy-bottomed, ovenproof casserole and fry the beef for about 4 minutes until nicely browned. Add the onion, garlic and mushrooms as well as the swede, leek, parsnip and potatoes and continue to brown for a further 4 minutes.

4 Stir in the tomato sauce (or tomatoes) and stock and add the bay leaf. Bring to the boil, cover and transfer to the middle of the oven. Bake for about 1½ hours or until the vegetables are tender. Leave to cool in the pan.

5 When cool, remove the bay leaf and discard. Strain the casserole over a bowl and reserve the cooking liquid.

6 Whiz the meat and vegetables in a food processor, adding the reserved liquid to reach the correct texture. Alternatively, just mash the mixture for older babies. Divide into portions, then serve or freeze.

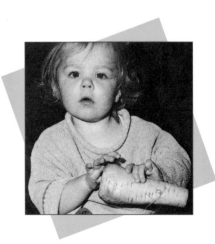

coco's simple bolognese

Any shape of pasta will do if you are going to whiz it in a food processor for a small baby. As your child gets older, you can add interest by using different small pasta shapes – the shaped pasta you can buy these days are great fun. It is very important, from the age of seven to nine months, to encourage your baby to chew and get used to textures. Studies show if children get used to chewing early on, they won't grow up to be fussy eaters!

Makes: 6–8 portions

14oz/400g fresh tomato sauce (see page 122) or 1 x 14oz/400g tin chopped tomatoes
4oz/100g pasta (any shape)
1 tablespoon/15ml sunflower oil
1 small onion, peeled and chopped
10oz/275g lean minced beef
½ pint/275ml unsalted beef stock (see page 124)
1 bay leaf

1 Prepare the fresh tomato sauce and set aside.

3 Cook the pasta according to the package instructions, but do not add any salt. When cooked, rinse with water, then drain.

4 Heat the oil in a pan and fry the onion and the beef mince for 6 to 8 minutes until brown. Stir in the tomato sauce (or chopped tomatoes) and stock and add the bay leaf. Bring to the boil and reduce the heat. Simmer for about 40 minutes and remove from the heat.

5 When cool, remove the bay leaf and discard. Add the pasta and whiz in a food processor, or leave chunky for older children. Divide into portions, then serve or freeze.

nutritional info

Tomatoes are rich in beta-carotene and lycopene, which work with vitamin C to make powerful antioxidants, known to prevent certain cancers.

Pasta is packed with carbohydrates and therefore provides good fuel for active children.

gourmet coco

Please don't let the word "gourmet" put you off; it only takes a little more time to create these extra special meals for your baby.

This range of more sophisticated recipes, using a wide variety of ingredients, will give your baby the opportunity to try all sorts of textures and flavours. Bear in mind that our children are the future generation of parents, shoppers and restaurant customers, so teaching them from a young age to appreciate different flavours and textures is giving them a good start.

Don't be afraid to be adventurous! Coco is, and she adores all these recipes!

spicy cauliflower with cumin

I made this dish for the family as part of a curry. Coco, being her usual self, wanted to try some – it was a little hot for her, but she loved it, so I have adjusted the recipe to suit the younger palate.

Cumin is similar to caraway, with a more savoury, hot taste. It is the dried fruit of a plant related to the parsley family. Use it sparingly as it can be quite spicy!

Makes: 6–8 portions

2–3 medium (about 10oz/275g) potatoes, for mash
14oz/400g fresh tomato sauce (see page 122) or 1 x 14oz/400g tin chopped tomatoes
1 cauliflower (about 1lb/450g), cut into florets
1oz/25g unsalted butter
1 tablespoon/15ml sunflower oil
1 small onion, peeled and chopped
1 clove garlic, peeled and chopped
¼ teaspoon powdered cumin

1 Prepare the potato mash (see page 121) and the fresh tomato sauce; set aside.

2 Put the cauliflower in a saucepan with rapidly boiling water. Cook, uncovered, for about 15 minutes or until tender and strain.

3 Heat the butter and oil in a pan and gently fry the onion and garlic for about 3 minutes. Add the tomato sauce (or chopped tomatoes) and cumin and simmer for a further 5 minutes.

4 Place the tomato mixture and the cauliflower in a food processor and whiz, or leave chunky for older children. Add to the mashed potato. Leave to cool, then divide into portions and serve or freeze.

nutritional info

Cauliflower is rich in beta-carotene and folic acid and contains small amounts of B vitamins, calcium, magnesium and phosphorous. It also has cancer-fighting glucosinolates.

lemon sole with vegetables in a cheesy sauce

It is so important to give your baby fish – people are sometimes afraid of cooking fish, but it really couldn't be easier!

Lemon sole has a lovely delicate flavour with only one main bone to remove. It is much softer and more delicate than Dover sole, and also costs less. Alternatively, you can use plaice.

Makes: 6–8 portions

2–3 medium potatoes (about
   10oz/275g), for mash
1 small carrot (about 2oz/50g), peeled
   and sliced
2oz/50g French beans
2oz/50g frozen peas
1 pint/570ml unsalted fish stock
   (see page 125)
8oz/225g lemon sole, skinned and
   boned
¼ pint/150ml white sauce (see
   page 121)
2oz/50g hard cheese, grated

1 Prepare the potato mash (see page 121) and set aside.

2 Put the sliced carrot into a saucepan, with enough water to cover and bring to the boil. Cook, covered, for 12 minutes until tender; strain and set aside. Put the French beans into a saucepan of rapidly boiling water and cook for 4 to 5 minutes, strain and set aside. Put the peas into a saucepan with rapidly boiling water and cook for about 3 minutes; strain and set aside.

3 Put the stock in a pan and bring to simmering point. Poach the lemon sole for 3 to 5 minutes, depending on the thickness of the fish. When it is cooked through and firm to the touch, lift out and set aside.

4 Prepare the white sauce and whisk in the cheese until it is melted. Add the vegetables to the cheese sauce and flake in the fish. Blend in a food processor or leave chunky for older children, and add to the mashed potatoes. Leave to cool, then divide into portions and serve or freeze.

more about...
cheese

For this recipe I use Cheddar cheese because it is usually in my fridge, but any tasty hard cheese works. Just make sure you always buy pasteurized cheese. Any soft cheese is best avoided since it may contain listeria, the bacteria associated with food poisoning. Cheese is full of protein and calcium, good for healthy bones and teeth.

monkfish with mushrooms, broad beans, potato and winter savoury

I've used monkfish in this recipe as we usually have it in the restaurant. It's a lovely meaty fish with no tiny bones. It's also a rich source of essential proteins and is easily digested. But you can use cod instead.

Winter savoury is a herb with a hot and peppery flavour, so use it sparingly. It goes perfectly with beans and pulses. It aids digestion and stimulates the appetite. If you can't get it, use watercress instead.

Makes: 6–8 portions

4 medium potatoes (about 1lb/450g), for mash
6oz/175g fresh broad beans, shelled
3oz/75g unsalted butter
2 tablespoons/30ml olive oil
8oz/225g monkfish or cod, skinned and boned
8oz/225g button mushrooms, thinly sliced
2 sprigs winter savoury or a small bunch of watercress, washed and picked so as to remove the stalks
4fl oz/125ml baby's usual milk

1 Prepare the potato mash (see page 121) and set aside.

2 Meanwhile, put the broad beans into a saucepan of boiling water, bring back to the boil and cook until tender. This will take 4 to 5 minutes if they are young, longer if they are larger and older. Test one of the beans by peeling off the outer skin to see if the bean is tender. Rinse under cold water and strain. Peel off the outer skins of the beans – a bit of work but well worth it!

3 Heat 1oz/25g butter and 1 teaspoon/5ml oil in a pan. Fry the monkfish or cod for about 5 minutes, depending on thickness, until it is firm and opaque; set aside with its juices. Heat the remaining oil and butter and gently fry the mushrooms for about 5 minutes.

4 Put the monkfish and its juices together with the mushrooms, beans and winter savoury (or watercress) in the food processor and whiz, adding some of the milk. Add this mixture to the mashed potatoes, correcting the texture with more milk if necessary. Leave to cool, then divide into portions and serve or freeze.

terranean-style salmon

This is a fresh-tasting dish – full of "sunshine" and ideal for the entire family on a hot summer's day.

Makes: 6–8 portions

14oz/400g fresh tomato sauce (see page 122) or 1 x 14oz/400g tin chopped tomatoes
1 tablespoon/15ml sunflower oil
8oz/225g salmon fillet
1oz/25g unsalted butter
2oz/50g onion, peeled and finely diced
1 clove garlic, peeled and crushed
1 medium red pepper (about 4oz/100g), cored, seeded and finely diced
1 courgette (about 4oz/100g), finely diced
1 sprig fresh thyme
4 fresh basil leaves
1 bay leaf
3oz/75g pasta (small shapes)

1 Prepare the fresh tomato sauce and set aside.

2 Preheat the oven to 160ºC, 325ºF.

3 Heat a non-stick pan until quite hot. Add the oil and fry the salmon, flesh side down, for about 3 minutes. Turn over and fry for a further 3 minutes, then remove from the pan and set aside. When the salmon is cold, remove the skin and flake.

4 In an ovenproof pan, gently fry the onion, garlic, pepper and courgette in the butter, cover and cook over a gentle heat for about 8 minutes, stirring occasionally.

5 Stir in the tomato sauce (or chopped tomatoes) and herbs and bring to the boil. Add the salmon, cover and transfer to the oven. Cook for 8 to 10 minutes, making sure that the salmon is cooked through and the vegetables are tender. Remove the herbs and leave to cool.

6 Meanwhile, cook the pasta according to the package instructions, but do not add any salt. When cooked, rinse with water, then drain.

7 For older babies, simply mix the flaked salmon into the pasta and vegetables, or for younger ones, whiz the mixture in a food processor. Divide into portions, then serve or freeze.

more about...
bay

The leaf of an evergreen tree that belongs to the laurel family, bay is said to stimulate the appetite and to aid digestion. It is used to add flavour to fish, stews and the like, but it can also be used in sweet dishes. Martin uses it to flavour milk for his bay leaf crème brûlée.

...ached salmon with vegetables in creamy dill sauce

When you buy salmon, make sure the skin and bones have been removed, but run your fingers over the fish before you cook it to make doubly sure.

Makes: 6–8 portions

4 medium potatoes (about 1lb/450g), for mash
1 medium carrot (about 6oz/175g), peeled and chopped
8oz/225g salmon, skinned and boned
½ pint/275ml baby's usual milk
½ pint/275ml white sauce, made using the poaching milk
5 sprigs fresh dill, chopped
2oz/50g fresh or frozen peas

1 Prepare the potato mash (see page 121) and set aside.

2 In another saucepan, cook the carrot for about 12 minutes until tender and drain.

3 In a saucepan large enough to hold the fish, cover the fish with the milk. Bring to the boil and immediately reduce the heat. Simmer for about 5 minutes until the fish is firm to the touch. Remove the salmon, reserving the poaching milk.

4 Use the poaching milk to make the white sauce, adding the dill at the end.

5 Cook the peas for about 2 minutes and drain.

6 Whiz the carrots, salmon and peas together in a food processor and add some of the dill sauce to correct the texture. Add to the mashed potatoes, using more sauce as required. Leave to cool, then divide into portions and serve or freeze.

creamy chicken with mushrooms and beans

For older babies who can chew, leave the chicken, beans and mushrooms chunky instead of whizzing them in the food processor.

Makes: 6–8 portions

3 medium potatoes (about 12oz/350g), for mash
¼ pint/150ml white sauce
4oz/100g green beans
1oz/25g unsalted butter
1 tablespoon/15ml sunflower oil
1 small onion, peeled and chopped
2 boneless chicken breasts (about 10oz/275g), skinned and diced
2oz/50g button mushrooms, sliced
¼ pint/150ml unsalted chicken stock (see page 125)

1 Prepare the potato mash (see page 121) and the white sauce and set aside.

2 String, top and tail and slice the beans. Cook them in a saucepan of boiling water for 4 to 5 minutes or until tender; drain.

3 Heat the butter and oil in a pan and gently fry the onions for about 2 minutes. Add the chicken and mushrooms and cook for a further 2 minutes. Stir in the chicken stock and white sauce and bring to the boil. Reduce the heat and simmer for about 10 minutes until the chicken is cooked. Strain over a bowl and reserve the sauce.

4 Add the beans to the chicken and whiz in a food processor. Add the chicken mixture to the mashed potatoes, adding sauce to correct the texture if necessary. Leave to cool, then divide into portions and serve or freeze.

Chicken and sweetcorn velouté with rice

This is a simple dish, but very tasty, because you use all the flavours from the chicken stock in the sauce.

I use this recipe when I make chicken pie for the family. Add any vegetables you like and simply put the cooked chicken and vegetables in a pie dish, cover with the velouté sauce and then cover with pastry – shop-bought is fine! Pop it in the oven and serve with rice or . potatoes.

Makes: 6–8 portions

2 chicken legs (about 12oz/350g), skinned
1 pint/570ml unsalted chicken stock (see page 125)
1 bay leaf
5oz/150g long-grain rice
2oz/50g frozen sweetcorn kernels
¼ pint/150ml velouté sauce, using the reserved stock

1 Put the chicken in a saucepan with the stock and the bay leaf, bring to the boil and cover. Reduce the heat and gently simmer for about 40 minutes or until the chicken is tender. Leave to cool. Remove the chicken from the stock and take the meat off the bone, but reserve the stock.

2 Boil the rice according to the package instructions, but do not add any salt; drain.

3 Cook the sweetcorn in a saucepan of boiling water for about 3 minutes; drain.

4 Strain the stock into a clean pan and leave to cool. Make the velouté sauce using the same method as for basic white sauce (see page 121), but using the stock instead of milk.

5 Blend the chicken, sweetcorn and rice in the food processor, adding a little sauce at a time, or leave chunky for older children. Leave to cool, then divide into portions and serve or freeze.

more about...
velouté sauce

A velouté sauce is made using stock instead of milk, so you use all the flavour and goodness of the chicken in the sauce. You will only need about ¼ pint/150ml sauce, but you can freeze the rest when it is cold.

chicken with lemon and rosemary

This is so easy. Once you have all the ingredients together, simply put it in the oven!

Don't be afraid to introduce herbs to your baby's diet – it gives them a chance to taste exciting new flavours. The rosemary goes really well with the lemon and chicken – you'll see.

Makes: 6–8 portions

3 medium potatoes (about 12oz/350g),
   for mash
1 medium carrot (about 4oz/100g),
   peeled and diced
2 chicken legs (about 12oz/350g),
   skinned
1 sprig rosemary
1 small onion, peeled and chopped
½ pint/275ml unsalted chicken stock
   (see page 125)
Juice of ½ small lemon

1 Prepare the potato mash (see page 121) and set aside.

2 In a saucepan, cook the carrot for about 12 minutes until tender and drain in a colander.

3 Preheat the oven to 170°C, 325°F.

4 Put the chicken in an ovenproof pan with the rosemary and onion. Add the stock, bring to the boil and cover. Transfer to the oven and cook for about 40 minutes, or until the chicken is tender.

5 Leave to cool in the pan, then strain the chicken over a bowl, reserving the cooking liquid.

6 Take the meat off the bone and put into a food processor with the lemon juice, also adding the onion and carrots. Blend, leaving it more chunky for older children. Add to the mashed potatoes, adding more stock if necessary. Divide into portions, then serve or freeze.

braised pork with apricots

This sounds like a grown-up dish, but it is suitable for little ones as well. The apricots give it a lovely tangy flavour, which works really well with the pork. Coco usually picks out all the apricot pieces first. You can serve this dish with noodles, rice or potatoes.

nutritional info

Leeks are high in the B vitamins, biotin and vitamin C, as well as being rich in calcium. Onions and leeks both help us to process fatty foods, and so help in cutting cholesterol.

Apricot is a high-energy dried fruit, rich in potassium, promoting healthy nerves and muscles.

Makes: 6–8 portions

10oz/275g shoulder of pork, finely diced
2 tablespoons/15g flour
1oz/25g unsalted butter
1 tablespoon/15ml sunflower oil
1 small onion, peeled and chopped
1 medium carrot (about 4oz/100g), peeled and finely diced
1 medium leek (about 4oz/100g), chopped
1 pint/570ml unsalted chicken or pork stock (see page 125)
1 bay leaf
2 fresh apricots (or 4 dried and soaked), chopped

1 Preheat the oven to 160°C, 325°F.

2 Dust the pork with the flour. Put the butter and oil into a heavy-bottomed, ovenproof pan over a medium heat. Add the pork and fry for about 5 minutes until brown. Add the onion, carrot and leek and continue to brown for a further 4 minutes.

3 Cover with the stock, add the bay leaf and bring to the boil. Cover, transfer to the oven and cook for about 1 hour. Add the apricots and cook in the oven for a further 15 minutes or until tender.

4 Leave to cool and remove the bay leaf. Blend in a food processor or leave chunky for older children. Divide into portions and serve or freeze.

pork fillet with mushrooms, egg noodles and a soy-flavoured sauce

We were invited to friends of ours who had cooked a Chinese meal. I had taken a portion of Coco's own food with me, just in case, but she was happy picking out noodles, pork and mushrooms.

Here is a simpler version of what we had, giving you the opportunity to introduce some Oriental flavours such as ginger and soy sauce. This is a really quick and easy recipe.

Makes: 6–8 portions

8oz/225g pork fillet, trimmed of fat
1 tablespoon/15ml sunflower oil
½ teaspoon fresh ginger, grated
¼ pint/150ml unsalted chicken stock
  (see page 125)
1 dessertspoon/10ml soy sauce
1oz/25g unsalted butter
½ small onion, peeled and chopped
2oz/50g mushrooms, finely sliced
4oz/100g egg noodles

1 Cut the pork fillet into slices and then into small strips. Heat a non-stick pan until very hot. Fry the pork strips in the oil for about 3 minutes until brown and cooked through. Add the ginger, stock and soy sauce, bring to the boil and remove the pan from the heat.

2 In another pan, gently fry the onions in the butter for about 2 minutes, add the mushrooms and fry for a further 2 minutes. Add to the pork.

3 Cook the noodles in boiling water for about 3 minutes, drain and add to the pork. Leave to cool and whiz in a food processor, or leave chunky for older babies. Divide into portions and serve or freeze.

"simply scrumptious"

gammon and pineapple

I remember my grandparents taking us out for lunch when I was a little girl. My grandfather always had this classic dish, so I thought it was very grown-up and followed suit. The sweetness of the pineapple really complements the gammon.

Even after soaking, gammon can be salty, so this recipe is better suited to babies older than twelve months.

Makes: 6–8 portions

3–4 medium potatoes (about
   14oz/400g), for mash
8oz/225g gammon steak, soaked
   overnight in cold water
1oz/25g unsalted butter
1 tablespoon/15ml sunflower oil
3 pineapple slices, diced, plus juice
   (not syrup) from 1 x 8oz/220g tin
About 3 tablespoons/45ml water

1 Prepare the potato mash (see page 121) and set aside.

2 Remove any fat from the gammon and cut into small cubes. Quickly fry the gammon pieces in the butter and oil, add the pineapple, its juice and the water and cook for about 5 minutes until the gammon is done, adding more water if necessary.

3 Cool and blend for younger babies and add to the mashed potato. For older babies just add the chunks of gammon and pineapple to the mash. Divide into portions and serve or freeze.

preparation tip

Gammon can be salty, so make sure you soak it to remove some of the salt. To soak, put the gammon in a large saucepan and cover with cold water. Leave overnight, changing the water regularly if possible.

lamb with leeks and carrots in a tomato and rosemary sauce

You can, if you wish, use a cheaper cut of lamb such as leg steak, but it may take longer to cook.

Makes: 6–8 portions

14oz/400g fresh tomato sauce (see page 122) or 1 x 14oz/400g tin chopped tomatoes

1 tablespoon/15ml sunflower oil

8oz/225g loin of lamb (trimmed weight), cubed

1 tablespoon/10g plain flour

1 small onion, peeled and chopped

1 clove garlic, peeled and crushed

1 small leek (about 2oz/50g), peeled and chopped

1 medium carrot (about 6oz/175g), peeled and diced

2 medium potatoes (about 8oz/225g), peeled and diced

¾ pint/425ml unsalted vegetable or lamb stock (see page 125)

1 small sprig of rosemary

1 Prepare the fresh tomato sauce and set aside.

2 Preheat the oven to 160ºC, 325ºF.

3 Heat the oil in an ovenproof casserole dish. Dust the lamb with the flour and fry for about 5 minutes until well browned. Add the onion, garlic, leek, carrot and potatoes and fry for a further 4 minutes.

4 Stir in the tomato sauce (or tomatoes), stock and rosemary and bring to the boil. Cover and transfer to the oven. Cook for about 1¼ hours, or until tender. Remove from the oven and leave to cool in the casserole dish.

5 Remove the rosemary, strain and reserve the cooking liquid. Whiz in a food processor, adding the cooking liquid to adjust the texture as required. For older babies you can mash the mixture or leave it chunky. Divide into portions, then serve or freeze.

more about...
rosemary

Rosemary is one of the most popular herbs used in cooking, especially with meats and fish, and also to flavour oils. It is known to help with digestion.

lamb and aubergine bake

Lamb and aubergines go together really well. The aubergine has a lovely creamy texture that adds moisture to the dish.

Makes: 6–8 portions

1oz/25g unsalted butter
1 tablespoon/15ml sunflower oil
8oz/225g lean lamb leg steak, cubed
1 onion, peeled and chopped
1 clove garlic, peeled and crushed
2 tablespoons/30ml aubergine purée (see page 16)
4fl oz/125ml unsalted vegetable stock (see page 125)
6oz/175g carrot and turnip purée (see page 16)

1 Preheat the oven to 160°C, 325°F.

2 Heat the butter and oil in a non-stick ovenproof pan and brown the lamb for about 5 minutes. Add the onion and garlic and gently fry for a further 4 minutes. Add the aubergine purée and stock and bring to simmering point.

3 Transfer the pan to the oven and cook, uncovered, for about 1 hour until the lamb is tender and the sauce is thick. Leave to cool in the pan.

4 Whiz in a food processor for younger babies, or leave chunky for older ones. Add the carrot and turnip purée. Divide into portions, then serve or freeze.

more about...
aubergines

Aubergines are available in different shapes and sizes and can range in colour from deep purple to white. They are available all year round and make an ideal baby food when cooked as they are.

There is no need to salt aubergines, unless they are home-grown and you need to get rid of any bitterness.

meatballs in tangy tomato sauce

Most children like meatballs. I make tiny little ones for Coco – she likes to use her fork to pick them up. What she doesn't realise, though, is that they also encourage her to chew.

Makes: 6–8 portions

For the meatballs:
2oz/50g fresh bread
1 small onion, peeled and chopped
12oz/350g beef (such as shin), finely diced
1 egg, beaten
1 tablespoon/15ml sunflower oil

For the sauce:
14oz/400g fresh tomato sauce (see page 122) or 1 x 14oz/400g tin chopped tomatoes
1 tablespoon/15ml sunflower oil
1 small onion, peeled and chopped
1 clove garlic, peeled and crushed
½ pint/275ml unsalted beef stock (see page 124)
½ teaspoon Italian herbs
1 bay leaf

To make the meatballs

1 Put the bread and onion into a food processor and whiz until the bread is reduced to crumbs. Add the beef and a little egg and whiz again, adding more egg if necessary. Form into balls – the size is up to you.

2 Heat the oil in a pan and gently fry the meatballs for about 5 minutes. Transfer them to an ovenproof dish.

To make the sauce

3 Prepare the fresh tomato sauce and set aside.

4 Gently fry the onion and garlic in the oil without colouring. Stir in the stock, tomato sauce (or tomatoes), herbs and bay leaf and bring to the boil. Pour over the meatballs and simmer, covered, for about 30 minutes.

5 Remove the bay leaf. Leave the sauce to cool, then whiz or mash. Divide into portions and serve or freeze.

serving tip

Serve the meatballs with rice, noodles or small shaped pasta. They are also delicious with mashed potatoes.

coco's simple stroganoff

Stroganoff is a classic Russian dish. The beef is always cut into strips. It is usually made with soured cream, but I have used double cream instead – the choice is up to you. Just remember not to boil the sauce once you have added the cream or it will separate. Serve with rice for an authentic taste.

Makes: 6–8 portions

1oz/25g unsalted butter
2 tablespoons/30ml sunflower oil
1 onion, peeled and chopped
4oz/100g mushrooms, sliced
10oz/275g sirloin beef steak, cut into
   thin strips
1 clove garlic, peeled and crushed
¼ pint/150ml unsalted beef stock
   (see page 124)
2fl oz/55ml double cream
¼ teaspoon grated nutmeg
1 tablespoon chopped parsley

1 Heat the butter and half the oil in a pan and gently fry the onion for about 3 minutes or until soft. Add the mushrooms and fry for a further 3 minutes; set aside.

2 Heat the remainder of the oil in a non-stick pan until very hot. Quickly brown the beef, then add the mushroom mixture, garlic and stock, and boil over a high heat for 2 minutes to reduce. Remove from the heat and add the cream, nutmeg and parsley.

3 Leave to cool, then blend in a food processor, or leave chunky for older babies. Divide into portions and serve or freeze.

"Mmmmore!"

omi's meatball soup

This is a typical Latvian dish. The recipe was given to me by Martin's mum who used to make it for Leon and Max when they were little; they love it and no matter how many times I make it, it is "never as good as Omi's". Coco loves it too.

Makes: 6–8 portions

For the meatballs:
2 slices white bread
3 tablespoons/45ml milk
1lb/450g lean beef mince (or half beef and half pork)
1 egg

For the soup:
1oz/25g unsalted butter
1 medium onion, peeled and diced
2 medium carrots (about 10oz/275g), peeled and diced
1¼ pint/725ml unsalted beef or vegetable stock (see page 124–125)
1 bay leaf
4 medium potatoes (about 1lb/450g), peeled and diced
1 sprig fresh dill, picked from the stalk and chopped

To make the meatballs

1 Place the bread in a shallow dish and pour the milk over. Leave to soak for a few minutes until absorbed, then squeeze out all the excess milk.

2 Put the mince into a bowl, add the bread and the egg and mix thoroughly until combined and smooth. (This can also be done in a food processor.)

3 Take about a dessertspoonful of the mince mixture and roll into a ball with the palms of your hands. Repeat until all of the mixture has been used. Leave the meatballs aside while you are preparing the soup.

To make the soup

4 Melt the butter in a pan and gently fry the onion and carrots for about 5 minutes. Stir in the stock, add the bay leaf and bring to the boil. Cook for about 10 minutes, then add the potatoes and cook for a further 10 minutes.

5 Add the meatballs, bring back to the boil and reduce the heat. Simmer for a further 10 minutes until the meat is completely cooked through. Add the dill.

6 Remove the bay leaf and discard. Simply mash and serve for an older child. For younger babies, strain the soup into a bowl and reserve the liquid. Whiz in a food processor, adding the reserved liquid to obtain the correct texture. Leave to cool, then divide into portions and serve or freeze.

anytime sweet things

The recipes in this chapter can be for breakfast or pudding, or even a snack in the afternoon. I have used a wide selection of fruits to give variety.

Most fruits are available all year round these days, but it's much better to use them when they are in season and bursting with flavour, especially soft fruit. It's so good to see children eating fruit – dried or fresh. Coco loves it!

Many of the recipes can be served either on their own or mixed with plain yoghurt or ice-cream. Be creative and try your own combinations.

fresh mango purée

Mangoes are sweet and have a really velvety texture. But make sure that the mango is ripe – if it is green, the end result will be coarse and tasteless. Ripe mangoes are soft to the touch, and have a great smell. Unripe mangoes are usually very hard and green.

Makes: 4 portions

1 peeled and stoned ripe mango (about 12oz/350g), sliced

Just put the mango pieces into a food processor and whiz – simple as that! Divide into portions and serve or freeze.

fresh custard

Home-made custard does not freeze well – it tends to go watery. If you don't want to make fresh custard, powdered is great – in fact, Leon and Max prefer commercial custard to mine! Great, eh?

Makes: 6–8 portions

½ pint/275ml baby's usual milk
4 drops vanilla essence or arôme, or
½ vanilla pod, cut in half lengthwise
and seeds scraped out
3 egg yolks
1 teaspoon cornflour
1 dessertspoon/10g caster sugar

1 Gently heat the milk in a pan, add the vanilla pod, if using, and bring to boiling point.

2 Mix the egg yolks, cornflour, sugar in a bowl and slowly pour the milk over, stirring all the time. Add the vanilla essence or arôme, if using.

3 Return the mixture to the pan and heat it gently, stirring for about 2 minutes, until it has thickened. If it looks grainy, take it off the heat and whisk – it will become smooth again. If using the vanilla pod, remove.

4 Divide into portions and serve, or keep in the fridge for 2 to 3 days, covered with cling film.

serving tip

Custard is good enough to have on its own, but try it with any of the fruit purées, turnovers or crumbles. It's delicious over a chocolate brownie fresh from the oven.

dried winter fruit compote

This is fantastic with porridge – simply mix a few spoons with your baby's usual baby porridge or baby cereal. You can buy mixed bags of dried fruit, but it's so easy to make up your own – pears, apples, apricots, peaches and prunes – but be sure all the stones have been removed.

Makes: 6–8 portions

1lb/450g mixed dried fruit

1 Soak the fruit in water overnight. Strain, cover with fresh water and cook for about 20 minutes. Leave to cool in the juice.

2 Strain the fruit over a bowl, reserving the juice. Purée in a food processor, adding juice to correct the texture, or leave chunky for older children. Divide into portions and serve or freeze.

compote of forest fruits

Some berry fruits may cause an allergic reaction in young babies. If there is a history of allergies in the family, remember to check with your health visitor first.

This dish is not suitable for younger babies because of the seeds, so give it after seven months. For younger babies you could blend the mixture in a processor, but you would also have to sieve it to remove the seeds, which might waste a lot.

Most supermarkets have a good selection of frozen berry fruits – so it is easy enough to keep a bag in the freezer. Cooking really brings out the flavours of the fruits. If you are pushed for time, serve this over ice-cream for a fast, tasty treat.

Makes: 6–8 portions

1lb/450g frozen fruits such as summer berries or fruits of the forest
Sugar to taste

Simply cook the fruit from frozen in a small saucepan. It takes 10 to 15 minutes for the fruits to defrost. Don't add any water but add a little sugar to taste. Divide into portions and serve or freeze.

preparation tip

You can freeze your own fruits when they are abundant in the summer. Martin spreads them out on a tray, puts them in the freezer and when frozen hard, parcels them in useful quantities into freezer bags.

custard apple with yoghurt and honey

Also called cherimoya, the custard apple has the texture of thick custard – hence its name. Once hard to find, it now appears on most supermarket shelves.

This recipe is a bit of work – there are a lot of shiny black seeds to remove – but the white flesh does taste fantastic and it is worth it.

Makes: 6–8 portions

3 ripe custard apples, peeled
6 tablespoons/90ml thick plain yogurt
1 teaspoon honey, preferably runny

1 Halve the fruits, scoop out the flesh and seeds into a sieve over a bowl and press the white flesh through the sieve with a spoon.

2 Add the yogurt and honey and mix well. Divide into portions, then serve or freeze.

caution

Honey should not be given to babies under 12 months because of the small risk of infant botulism – a rare form of food-poisoning.

honey and apricot

Dried apricot is a high-energy snack rich in potassium. Check the label to make sure the apricots have not been treated with sulphur dioxide (used to preserve the bright orange colour). If you can get semi-dried ready-to-eat apricots, use them – they are nicer.

Makes: 6–8 portions

10oz/275g dried apricots, soaked in
water overnight
1 dessertspoon honey

1 Put the apricots with the soaking liquid into a saucepan and add the honey. Gently cook for 6 to 8 minutes, uncovered.

2 Leave the apricots to cool in the syrup. Then whiz in a food processor. Divide into portions, then serve or freeze.

nutty fruit crumble

All the fruit purées in this book are suitable to use in a crumble, except for the custard apple. The oats give this crumble a lovely coarse and nutty texture.

Makes: 6–8 portions

4oz/100g plain flour
3oz/75g unsalted butter
2½oz/60g rolled oats
1½oz/40g ground almonds
2oz/50g caster sugar
4 drops vanilla essence or arôme
1½lb/750g fruit purée of your choice

1 Preheat the oven to 180°C, 350°F.

2 Sieve the flour into a mixing bowl. Rub the butter into the flour until it has a sandy texture. Add the oats, almonds, sugar and vanilla and mix in well.

3 Put the fruit purée in a pie dish and sprinkle the crumble mix over the fruit evenly.

4 Place in the oven for 25 to 30 minutes until the top is golden brown. Leave to cool, then divide into portions and serve or freeze.

variation

For an even quicker basic crumble mix, sieve 6oz/175g plain flour into a mixing bowl. Rub in 3oz/75g unsalted butter and then stir in 3oz/75g caster sugar. Again, use with about 1½lb/750g fruit purée of your choice.

banana and fresh date purée

This makes a wicked crumble if used in the recipe opposite! You don't need to add any sugar as the dates are naturally sweet. For babies younger than six months, you will definitely need to whiz the fruit in a food processor as the skins of the dates can be a little tough.

Makes: 6–8 portions

2 large bananas (about 9oz/250g), sliced
Juice of ½ lemon
2 tablespoons/30ml water
3oz/75g dates, stoned and roughly chopped

1 Place all the ingredients in a pan, cover and simmer over medium heat for about 8 minutes. Mash together.

2 Leave to cool, then divide into portions and serve or freeze.

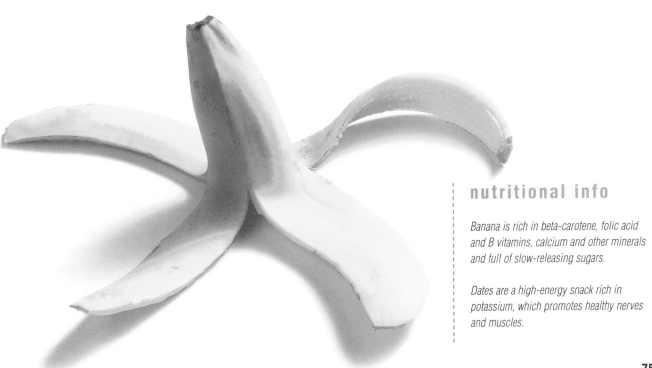

nutritional info

Banana is rich in beta-carotene, folic acid and B vitamins, calcium and other minerals and full of slow-releasing sugars.

Dates are a high-energy snack rich in potassium, which promotes healthy nerves and muscles.

75

quince purée

We are very lucky to have quince growing in the garden, so I have included this recipe. Quince has a delicious flavour. If you can't find quince, use a mix of apples and pears – it will give a similar result.

Makes: 6–8 portions

12oz/350g peeled and cored quince, diced
½oz/10g unsalted butter
2 tablespoons/30ml cold water
Juice of ½ lemon

1 Place the quince in a pan with the butter, water and lemon juice. Cover, bring to the simmer and cook for 30 to 40 minutes until tender.

2 Whiz into a purée in a food processor or with a hand-held blender. Leave to cool, then divide into portions and serve or freeze.

rhubarb purée

This is a fantastic purée, especially for crumble (see page 74), although it may be a little sharp for very young babies. Try to get champagne rhubarb if you can – it is forced and has a much more delicate flavour than the rhubarb grown without any cover in the garden, which can be thick, green and sharp.

Makes: 6–8 portions

1lb/450g champagne rhubarb, sliced
2oz/50g sugar

1 Put the rhubarb into a non-reactive, heavy-bottomed pan with the sugar. Cover and cook over a gentle heat for 15 to 20 minutes until the rhubarb is completely soft.

2 Strain over a bowl, cool and whiz in a food processor or with a hand-held blender if necessary.

3 Leave to cool, then divide into portions and serve or freeze.

preparation tip

You can add a cardamom pod to the rhubarb while it is cooking to give it a lovely scented flavour – but remember to remove it from the pan before you blend or serve! For more on cardamom, see Mango and Cardamom Purée on page 87.

blueberry, banana and apple purée

Blueberries are naturally sweet, very flavourful and go well with banana and apple. Try this recipe – you won't be disappointed!

Makes: 6–8 portions

8oz/225g blueberries
8oz/225g peeled and cored dessert
   apples, evenly sliced
1 banana (about 2oz/50g), sliced

1 Put all the fruit in a non-reactive, heavy-bottomed pan and cook slowly with the lid on, stirring now and again. No water is needed as the natural juices will come out of the fruit. After 5 minutes, take the lid off and simmer for about a further 5 minutes or until the juices have evaporated.

2 Leave chunky for older children or to use for pie filling or puffs, (see page 81). Purée for small babies or to use in a crumble (see page 74). Leave to cool, then divide into portions and serve or freeze.

caution

Blueberries may cause an allergic reaction in babies with a family history of allergies. If this is the case with your baby, check with your health visitor before you use this fruit.

apple, sultana & cinnamon purée

I use Cox's Orange Pippin apples, but you can also try Royal Gala. This can be eaten as is, or left slightly chunkier and used as the filling for puffs (see page 81).

Makes: 6–8 portions

8oz/225g peeled and cored apple,
   sliced
Juice of ½ lemon
2oz/50g sultanas
½ cinnamon stick or ½ teaspoon dried
   ground cinnamon

1 Combine the apple, lemon juice, sultanas and cinnamon in a non-reactive saucepan. Cover with a tight-fitting lid and bring to the simmer. Cook slowly, stirring from time to time. After 8 to 10 minutes, or when the fruit is tender, remove from the heat. Remove the cinnamon stick.

2 Purée the apple mixture in a food processor or with a hand-held blender. Leave to cool, then divide into portions and serve or freeze.

apple and cinnamon muffins

Any dessert apple will do – try Royal Gala, Red Delicious, Braeburn or Spartan. You can keep the muffins in an airtight tin for up to 2 days – but they probably won't last that long!

To get a good shape, use a muffin rather than a bun tin as it is deeper – it is also better to line it with paper cases. However, if you don't use paper cases, grease the tin lightly before adding the mixture. If you make smaller muffins, you will get up to fifteen from this recipe.

Makes: 10–12 muffins

9oz/250g plain flour
1 tablespoon/10g baking powder
3oz/75g sugar
1 teaspoon ground cinnamon
3fl oz/90ml milk
2fl oz/55ml apple juice
1 egg, beaten
3oz/75g unsalted butter, melted
5oz/150g dessert apple, peeled and
   chopped

1 Preheat the oven to 190ºC, 375ºF. Grease a muffin tin or line it with paper cases.

2 In a large bowl, sift together the flour, baking powder, sugar and cinnamon. In another bowl, combine the milk, apple juice, egg and butter.

3 Pour the wet ingredients into the bowl of dry ingredients and stir until just combined. Be careful not to overstir – this batter has quite a thick consistency as the apple will give out juices as it cooks. Add the chopped apple and stir again once or twice.

4 Spoon the batter into the muffin tins and bake for 20 to 25 minutes until brown. Remove from the oven and allow to cool in the tin.

blueberry and lemon muffins

I use the semi-dried blueberries available in most supermarkets, but it's great to use fresh berries when they are available. You can also replace the lemon with orange.

Try to use an unwaxed lemon or orange, but if you can't find any, remember to wash the fruit first to remove any wax. When zesting, take care not to include any of the white pith, as it is bitter.

You can keep these muffins in an airtight tin for up to two days.

Makes: 10–12 muffins

10oz/275g plain flour
1 tablespoon/10g baking powder
Pinch of salt
7fl oz/210ml milk
1 egg, beaten
1fl oz/30ml lemon juice
4oz/100g caster sugar
3oz/75g unsalted butter, melted
6oz/175g semi-dried or fresh
  blueberries
1 teaspoon grated lemon zest

1 Preheat the oven to 190°C, 375°F. Grease a muffin tin or line it with paper cases.

2 In a mixing bowl, sift together the flour, baking powder and salt. In another bowl, combine the milk, egg, lemon juice, sugar and butter.

3 Pour all the wet ingredients into the dry ones and stir just enough to combine. The batter will be slightly lumpy. Fold in the berries at the end, but be careful not to overmix.

4 Spoon the batter into the muffin tin and bake for about 25 minutes until light brown. Remove from the oven and allow to cool in the tins.

"the kids love them, and so does Daddy"

fruity cinnamon puffs

Max thinks these fruity treats are lush; Coco is a great fan too! Be careful and don't be tempted to tuck into them when they come straight out of the oven – the filling is extremely hot! Serve the puffs on their own, or with thick cream or custard.

Makes: 8–10 puffs

8oz/225g puff pastry, home-made or
    bought
8oz/225g apple, sultana and
    cinnamon purée (see page 77)
1 medium egg, beaten
A little caster sugar

1   On a lightly floured surface, roll out the pastry to a thickness of about ⅛in/3mm. Then, using a 3¾in/10cm round cutter, cut out as many discs as you can (you should get about 8 to 10).

2   Place a heaped teaspoon of apple purée in the centre of each pastry disc. Brush the edges with the beaten egg, fold the discs in half and seal well by crimping with your fingers or using the tines of a fork dipped in flour. Brush the puffs with the remaining beaten egg and sprinkle with a little caster sugar.

3   At this point, you can either bake or freeze the puffs. If you are not going to freeze them, you need to let the puffs rest in the fridge for at least 1 hour because they will burst open if you bake them straight away. Bake in an oven preheated to 190ºC, 375ºF, for 10 to 15 minutes or until golden brown.

4   To freeze, place them on a tray and put in the freezer. Bake from frozen by placing the tray in an oven preheated to 190ºC, 375ºF. Bake for 20 to 25 minutes or until golden brown.

5   Remove the puffs from the oven and allow to cool on the tray before you serve them.

baked pears in maple syrup

These baked pears are fantastic served with ice-cream, but are also delicious on their own.

Makes: 6–8 portions

4 ripe, firm pears, peeled
Juice of 1 orange
2 tablespoons/30ml maple syrup

1 Preheat the oven to 190ºC, 375ºF.

2 Remove the pear stalks and cut the pears in half. With a teaspoon, scoop out the cores.

3 Put the orange juice and maple syrup into a non-reactive, ovenproof pan and bring to the boil. Remove from the heat. Put the pears into the pan with the orange juice and maple syrup mixture and coat all over to stop the pears from going brown.

4 Bake, uncovered, for 25 to 30 minutes, coating the pears now and again with the juice and syrup mixture. When soft, lift the pears out onto a plate.

5 Reduce the sauce over high heat until sticky. Pour over the pears and leave to cool.

6 Depending on your baby's age, purée in a food processor, mash or chop. Divide into portions and serve or freeze.

"sticky and yummy"

more about...
maple syrup

The processed sap of the maple tree, maple syrup has a distinctive taste and I much prefer it to golden syrup. Try to get the real thing – not maple-flavoured syrup, which is also available.

rice pudding

It is important that you use short-grain rice, also known as pudding rice. It has a fatter shape and softer texture and is more sticky than long-grain rice, making it more suitable for pudding.

Although this is delicious plain, your baby may enjoy it combined with a fruit purée. Coco's favourite is apricot. Wait until the pudding has cooled before adding the purée.

Makes: 6–8 portions

Knob of unsalted butter
2oz/50g pudding rice
1 pint/570ml baby's usual milk
2oz/50g caster sugar
2–3 drops vanilla essence or arôme

Oven method

1 Preheat the oven to 160°C, 325°F.

2 Butter the sides and base of an ovenproof dish. Place all the ingredients in the dish and mix well. Cover with foil and put on the middle shelf of the oven. Cook for 1½ to 2 hours, stirring once or twice.

Microwave method

1 Butter the sides and base of a non-metallic bowl or dish. Add the remaining ingredients and mix well.

2 Transfer the container to the microwave oven. Set to high and cook, uncovered, for 10 minutes (in a 600 watt oven, less in a higher powered oven). Stir well and repeat a further three times for a total of 40 minutes.

3 Remember that with both of these cooking methods the finished dish is very, very hot. Allow to cool, then divide into portions and serve or freeze.

variation

Chocolate rice pudding
Prepare the rice pudding as above, but while still warm, stir in 2oz/50g grated chocolate. This can be served warm or chilled.

poached pears

This is especially yummy with vanilla ice-cream, but just as good on its own. It's also delicious served with Raspberry Sauce (see page 88). I prefer to use Conference or Comice pears.

Makes: 6–8 portions

4 ripe pears, peeled and quartered
Juice of ½ lemon
Sugar to taste

1 Use a teaspoon to scoop out the cores of the pears. Put in a saucepan, cover with water and add the lemon juice and a little sugar to taste. Gently poach, covered, for about 5 minutes, or until the fruit is tender.

2 Leave the pears to cool in the syrup. When cold, chop into small pieces, or whiz in a food processor for younger babies.

3 Divide into portions and serve or freeze.

pear condé

Both the main ingredients in this are easy to digest, which makes it an ideal dessert from early on.

Makes: 6–8 portions

1 quantity rice pudding (see page 84)
1 quantity poached pears (see left)
A little of baby's usual milk, or cream

1 Prepare the rice pudding.

2 Prepare the poached pears, but do not purée them. Chop the pears into small pieces.

3 Add the pears to the cold rice pudding, mixing in a little milk or cream to give a creamy texture. Divide into portions, chill in the fridge for 30 minutes, then serve or freeze.

semolina pudding with caramelised bananas

This is a delicious pudding and so simple to make. It brings back lovely memories of Sunday lunches when I was a child. Dad was a surgeon and was usually "on call", so it was rare that we sat down together as a family for a meal. But Sunday lunches were sacred – and semolina pudding was often part of them. Mum used to put a good dollop of jam in the middle of the semolina – can't beat it!

Makes: 6–8 portions

For the caramelised bananas:
1oz/25g unsalted butter
2oz/50g light demerara sugar
2 tablespoons/30ml water
2 bananas, sliced

For the semolina:
1 pint/570ml baby's usual milk
Knob of unsalted butter
2–3 drops vanilla essence or arôme
2oz/50g semolina
2oz/50g sugar

To make the caramelised bananas

1 Melt the butter in a pan with the sugar and water, stirring all the time. When the mixture starts bubbling, add the sliced bananas. Beware! The syrup is extremely hot and can give a nasty burn.

2 Cook the bananas for 5 to 8 minutes, depending on their ripeness, until soft. Leave to cool in the syrup.

To make the semolina

3 Place the milk and butter in a pan and heat it gently until the butter is melted. Add the vanilla essence.

4 Sprinkle in the semolina, stir and continue to heat gently until the milk boils and the mixture thickens. You may need to add a little more milk to get the correct consistency.

5 Cook for 2 to 3 minutes, reduce the heat and simmer for a further 5 minutes. Remove from the heat and stir in the sugar.

6 Stir the banana slices into the semolina and whiz the mixture in a food processor until smooth. Leave to cool, then divide into portions and serve or freeze.

preparation tip

After step 5, you could bake the finished semolina for about 30 minutes in the oven until lightly browned. Just pour the cooked semolina into an ovenproof dish and place in the middle of a moderate oven (200°C, 400°F).

warm strawberries with vanilla

Strawberries and vanilla is a fantastic combination. Serve it on its own, or with vanilla ice-cream, rice pudding or semolina. I prefer to make this dish when strawberries are in season, otherwise the fruit can be really sharp and watery.

Makes: 6–8 portions

1lb/450g strawberries, hulled
Seeds from 1 vanilla pod or 4 drops vanilla essence or arôme
Sugar to taste

1 Put the strawberries and vanilla seeds or essence in a heavy-bottomed saucepan, cover and cook slowly for about 10 minutes or until the strawberries are soft, depending on the ripeness of the strawberries. Add a little sugar to taste, if necessary.

2 For babies younger than six months, mash the strawberries or whiz them in a food processor or with a hand-held blender. Allow to cool, then divide into portions and serve or freeze.

warm mango and cardamom purée

A taste of the Orient! Cardamom has a pungent citrus flavour. Green cardamom is more delicate than black, which has a more earthy taste – for this dish I prefer the former. This is a fantastic purée to have with Rice Pudding (see page 84) or as a dip for Deep-fried Rice Pudding Balls (see page 111).

Makes: 6–8 portions

1 ripe mango (about 12oz/350g), peeled, stoned and chopped
Juice of 1 orange
1 cardamom pod

1 Place the mango in a pan with the orange juice and cardamom pod. Cover and cook gently for about 8 minutes, depending on the ripeness of the mango, until tender.

2 Leave to cool, remove the cardamom pod and whiz in a food processor or with a hand-held blender. Divide into portions, then serve or freeze.

poached peaches

raspberry sauce

peach melba

These are good plain or served with a dollop of vanilla ice-cream. It doesn't matter what variety of peach you use, as long as they're ripe.

Makes: 6–8 portions

4–6 ripe peaches
1½ tablespoons sugar

This sauce is delicious over vanilla ice-cream and can be used on top of most fruit purées for added flavour and colour.

Makes: 6–8 portions

12oz/350g fresh or defrosted
  raspberries
¼ pint/150ml water
Sugar to taste

If you've got the Poached Peaches, and you've got the Raspberry Sauce, it takes a matter of seconds to make peach melba. This classic combination works every time!

Makes: 8 portions

1 quantity raspberry sauce (see left)
1 quantity poached peaches (see left)

1 Place the peaches in a pan with the sugar, cover with water and simmer for about 10 minutes.

2 Strain off the syrup and leave the peaches to cool.

3 When cool, peel off the skins, stone and cut into small pieces for older children, or blend for babies. Divide into portions and serve or freeze.

1 Put the raspberries in a food processor with the water and blend until smooth.

2 Rub the mixture through a sieve to remove the seeds. Add sugar to taste and serve. Divide into portions and serve or freeze.

1 Prepare the raspberry sauce.

2 Prepare the poached peaches and cut into small pieces (or blend for smaller babies).

3 Pour the raspberry sauce over the peaches and serve chilled. This dish can also be frozen.

mascarpone and vanilla ice-cream

This is a very simple ice-cream for which you don't need an ice-cream maker. This is one of Martin's own recipes and an all-time favourite of mine. The balsamic vinegar may seem odd, but it cuts the richness of the cheese.

You can buy fantastic silicone moulds from kitchen shops – the one I have has eleven individual little moulds. You can use them to cook anything from Yorkshire puddings to muffins and buns. They're also great for small portions of purée or, in this case, ice-cream.

Makes: 6–8 portions

8oz/225g tub mascarpone cheese
2oz/50g caster sugar
⅛ pint/75ml single cream
1 teaspoon/5ml balsamic vinegar
2 tablespoons/30ml milk
4 drops vanilla essence or arôme

1 Using a hand-held blender or a food processor, mix all the ingredients together until smooth.

2 Pour the mixture into the moulds and freeze. When needed, remove the mould from the freezer and place in the fridge for about 20 minutes to soften before eating.

more about...
mascarpone

An Italian dessert cheese made from fresh cream, mascarpone is available from most supermarkets. It can be mixed with fresh fruit and a little sugar.

preparation tip

Why not create a ripple effect to add interest? It's easy to do and looks great! Simply add 4 tablespoons/60ml puréed warm strawberries with vanilla (see page 87) to the ice-cream mix before you put it in the freezer. Use a knife and give it a swirl, being careful not to stir too much and lose the ripple pattern.

missy independent

When the boys are at school, I don't usually eat a cooked lunch so it is handy to have some light bites in the freezer for Coco's lunch. Now she is beginning to want to feed herself, I've included lots of "finger food" ideas that let her experiment with her new-found independence. Many of these dishes can be frozen, but most are not suitable for blending.

Coco's favourite spreads and dips are very easy to make and you can change the herbs and flavours to suit your baby's taste. Experiment with different flavours – I use cream cheese, crème frâiche or plain yoghurt as the base.

There is nothing nicer than the smell of freshly baked cookies. Coco is of an age now where she loves mixing and stirring ingredients and making a mess, so I let her. Try some of her treats.

sweetcorn fritters

Unless you have an enormous pan, you'll have to cook these in batches. If you cram too many fritters in the pan at once, they will spread a little and then stick together.

Makes: 10–12 good-sized fritters

4oz/100g plain flour
¼ teaspoon baking powder
¼ teaspoon caster sugar
¼ teaspoon ground mace
1 egg, lightly beaten
3fl oz/90ml milk
2oz/50g tinned or frozen sweetcorn kernels
Unsalted butter or oil for frying

1 Sieve the dry ingredients into a bowl. Add the egg and about three-quarters of the milk. Mix well and add the remaining milk to make a smooth, thick batter. Mix in the sweetcorn.

2 Heat a little butter or oil in a non-stick pan, then spoon in the batter, a dessertspoonful at a time, frying gently for about 1½ minutes, until the surface appears silky. Turn over and continue cooking for about a further 1½ minutes until golden brown.

3 Lift out and lay on kitchen paper to cool. Repeat with the remaining mixture. Divide into portions and serve or freeze.

4 When needed, defrost and reheat for 5 to 10 minutes in an oven preheated to 180°C, 350°F.

"now I want to feed myself, please"

more about...
mace

The red-orange outer casing or bark of the nutmeg seed kernel, mace is similar in taste to nutmeg, but more refined. In this recipe you can use nutmeg if you don't have mace.

ham and cheese rockies

These little buns are named rockies because they look like rock cakes – not because they are hard! Coco and the boys love them warm with butter or cream cheese.

Chives are a gentle alternative to onions – they also stimulate the appetite.

Makes: 12 buns

6oz/175g self-raising flour
¼ teaspoon baking powder
3oz/75g unsalted butter
1½oz/40g hard cheese, finely grated
1oz/25g ham, finely chopped
1 dessertspoon chopped chives
6 tablespoons/90ml cold milk
1 egg, beaten

1 Preheat the oven to 200°C, 400°F.

2 Sift the flour and baking powder into a bowl. Rub in the butter until the mixture resembles fine breadcrumbs, then mix in the cheese, ham and chives.

3 Mix together the milk and egg, and add this egg mixture to the flour mixture to get a soft batter (dropping consistency).

4 Spoon the mix into a well buttered bun tin and bake for 20 to 25 minutes until well risen and golden brown.

preparation tip

To test if your batter has the right consistency, put some of the mixture on a spoon and turn the spoon upside down. The batter should fall off easily.

tuna and sweetcorn cakes

I use polenta to coat these instead of breadcrumbs – it makes them nice and crispy. As it is ground corn, polenta goes very well with sweetcorn. Coco loves tuna fish – it is tasty and easy to use.

Makes: 8 cakes

2 small potatoes (about 8oz/225g), for mash
3oz/75g frozen sweetcorn kernels
2 x 8oz/200g tins tuna fish in water or brine, drained
2 dessertspoons chopped parsley
Flour for coating
2 eggs, beaten
Polenta for coating
Oil for frying

1 Prepare the potato mash (see page 121) and set aside.

2 Cook the sweetcorn in boiling water for about 2 to 3 minutes and leave to cool. Rinse with cold water and drain.

3 Mix the tuna, sweetcorn, mashed potato and parsley. Divide the mixture into 8 cakes. (It will be quite crumbly so you will need to bring it together with the palms of your hands.)

4 Dip each cake into the flour, then the egg and then the polenta, and re-shape if necessary.

5 Place the cakes on a tray covered with cling film and put into the freezer. When frozen, transfer into freezer bags until needed.

6 To cook from frozen you can deep-fry (180°C/350°F), shallow-fry in a little oil, or grill for 5 to 6 minutes until piping hot inside.

preparation tip

If you are not going to freeze the cakes, you need to leave them to rest in the fridge for approximately an hour before frying or grilling them. Reduce the cooking time to 3 to 4 minutes.

93

salmon and parsley fish cakes

This recipe makes 12 dainty cakes – Coco generally eats two per portion.

Makes: 6 portions

2 small potatoes (about 8oz/225g), for mash
½oz/10g unsalted butter
8oz/225g fresh salmon fillet, skinned and pin-boned
1 small onion, peeled and roughly chopped
1 medium carrot, peeled and roughly chopped
6 black peppercorns
1 fresh bay leaf
1 tablespoon chopped parsley
Flour for dusting and coating
2 medium eggs beaten together with 1 tablespoon/15ml milk
Dried breadcrumbs (see page 123)

1 Prepare the potato mash (see page 121), beating in the butter while the potatoes are still hot. Then put the mixture into a mixing bowl.

2 Place the salmon fillet in a pan with the onion, carrot, pepper corns and bay leaf. Just cover with cold water. Bring to simmering point and poach for 4 to 5 minutes.

3 Cover the pan and remove from the heat, allowing the fish to cool in the pan. When cool, remove the salmon from the cooking liquid, pat dry with kitchen paper and gently flake into the bowl with the potatoes. Add the chopped parsley and mix.

4 Turn the mixture out onto a lightly floured board and form into a large sausage shape, about 12in/30cm by 2in/5cm. Cut evenly into 12 discs. Pat each disc with a little more flour, shaking off the excess, dip in the beaten egg and milk, then coat well with the breadcrumbs. Re-shape if necessary.

5 Place onto a suitable tray, cover with cling film and freeze. Once frozen, re-wrap in pairs.

6 When needed, deep-fry (180°C/350°F) from frozen for 5 to 6 minutes. (You can also shallow-fry in a little oil for 3 to 4 minutes each side.) Make sure the fish cakes are piping hot inside before serving them.

preparation tip

If you're not going to freeze the cakes, leave them to rest in the fridge for an hour before deep-frying them for 4 to 5 minutes.

goujons of fish

mango and lime mayonnaise

Delicious served with Mango and Lime Mayonnaise (see right). Alternatively, serve them with Fresh Red Pepper and Tomato Salsa (see page 99).

This is a great accompaniment to fried fish or chicken. Use shop-bought mayonnaise because it contains pasteurized eggs.

Be careful never to use raw or undercooked eggs in cooking for babies because they may contain salmonella bacteria, which can cause serious illness.

Makes: 26 goujons

8oz/225g white fish such as sole or cod, skinned and boned
Flour for dusting
2 eggs, beaten
Dried breadcrumbs (see page 123)

Makes: ½ pint/275ml

1 ripe mango, peeled and stoned
Juice of 1 lime
2 tablespoons/30ml mayonnaise

1 Cut the fish into ⅓in/1cm strips and dust with flour. Dip the fish strips in the beaten egg and then in breadcrumbs. Freeze flat on a tray. When frozen the strips can be wrapped into portions – I use about four to five per portion.

2 When needed, deep-fry from frozen (180ºC/350ºF) for about 3 to 4 minutes until piping hot. If you are not going to freeze, deep-fry the fish strips for 2 to 3 minutes.

1 Cut the mango flesh into chunks. Blend the mango and lime juice in a food processor, or use a hand-held blender.

2 Mix the mango and lime juice with the mayonnaise and leave for a few hours in the fridge for the flavours to develop. If you don't use all of it in one go, it will keep in the fridge for up to 3 days in a jar.

pork, apple and mint burgers

The mixture is a little wet but the end result is a lovely, moist burger. This recipe makes 16 to 18 little burgers – I usually give Coco 2 per portion.

This is another great dish for all the family. It is one of my favourites because it is both very tasty and very low in fat, which a lot of burgers aren't. The apples give it a lot of moisture and the parsley and mint add great flavour. These burgers also go very well with the Tzatziki (see page 108).

Makes: 8–9 portions

5oz/150g apples, peeled, cored and
   roughly chopped
1 tablespoon fresh shredded mint
1 tablespoon fresh shredded parsley
1 small onion, peeled
Juice of ½ lemon
1lb/450g minced pork
2oz/50g fresh breadcrumbs (see
   page 123)
Butter or oil for frying

1 Put the apples, mint, parsley, onion and lemon juice in a food processor and blend to a rough purée. Add the pork and breadcrumbs and blend again until smooth.

2 Shape the mixture into 8 or 9 small burgers. At this point you can either freeze them or fry them.

3 To freeze, lay them on a tray lined with cling film. Cover the burgers with another layer of cling film and put in the freezer. When they are frozen, you can wrap them into portions. When needed, defrost in the fridge overnight.

4 Heat some butter or oil in a pan and fry the burgers for 3 to 4 minutes each side until cooked through.

coco burgers

It is so easy to make your own burgers. That way you know exactly what is in them – a lot of shop-bought burgers contain additives and salt and are high in fat and bread to bulk them out.

Serve these with Fran's Fluffy Chips (see page 99).

Makes: 8 burgers

1 small onion, peeled
8oz/225g lean minced beef
4 tablespoons fresh breadcrumbs (see page 123)
1 small egg
Butter or oil for frying

1 Put the onion in the processor and chop. Add the beef, breadcrumbs and egg and whiz.

2 Form the mixture into 8 little burgers. At this point you can either freeze them or fry them.

3 To freeze, lay them on a tray lined with cling film. Cover the burgers with another layer of cling film and put in the freezer. When they are frozen, you can wrap them individually. When needed, defrost in the fridge overnight.

4 Heat some butter or oil in a pan and fry the burgers for 3 to 4 minutes each side until cooked through.

nutritional info

Beef is an excellent source of iron, which growing children need. Iron helps to transport oxygen and carbon dioxide to the blood cells. Beef is also high in protein.

Eggs are an excellent source of protein, for building and repairing body tissues. Eggs are rich in iron, phosphorous and zinc, and contain vitamins A, D and E.

fran's fluffy chips

By boiling the potatoes first, you ensure that the chips are fluffy and crisp. Credit for these goes to Fran, one of Martin's commis chefs. They always go down well with Coco and with the restaurant staff!

Makes: 4 portions

**2 large potatoes (about 12oz/350g), cut into large, equally
  sized wedges**
A little salt for sprinkling (optional)

1 Soak the potato wedges in cold water for about 20 minutes to get rid of some of the starch.

2 Bring a large saucepan of water to the boil, add the chips and bring back to the boil. Cook for 10 to 15 minutes until nearly cooked through. Strain and leave in the pan to steam for a further 10 minutes.

3 Deep-fry the chips (180°C/350°F) for 5 to 8 minutes, or until cooked. Sprinkle with a little salt, to stop them from going soggy, and serve. These are not suitable for freezing.

fresh red pepper and tomato salsa

So simple, but this is fantastic with Fran's Fluffy Chips (see left) and the Goujons of Fish (see page 95). The salsa will keep in an airtight container in the fridge for two to three days, and can also be frozen.

Makes: 4–6 portions

**1 large red pepper (about 7oz/200g), peeled, seeded and
  quartered**
1 small shallot or spring onion
1lb/450g fresh tomatoes, skinned, seeded and quartered
½ clove garlic, peeled
3 basil leaves
Squeeze of fresh lemon juice

Put all the ingredients into a food processor and whiz. Leave overnight to let the flavours intensify.

coco's light lunch omelette pancake

This is a very easy lunch, but Coco enjoys it as a light snack or for breakfast. Coco loves the part where I flip the omelette over like a pancake – I usually get a "Wheee!!!"

Cut the omelette into pieces of a size your baby will manage. This recipe is not suitable for freezing.

Makes: 1 portion

1 egg, beaten
1oz/25g cooked ham, finely diced
1oz/25g hard cheese, grated
Knob of unsalted butter

1 Mix the egg, ham and cheese in a bowl. Heat a non-stick pan. When the pan is hot, add the butter.

2 Add the egg mix, stir a little until it has set, 1 to 2 minutes, then flip over. Cook for a further few seconds and remove from the heat. Cut into pieces and serve.

caution

Remember to wash your hands after touching egg shells, as there can be salmonella bacteria on them, which can cause serious illness. Also wash the fork you have used to whisk the raw eggs.

dainty lamb and pumpkin cakes

Lamb mince on its own can be quite dry, but the pumpkin mash makes these little cakes really moist. Lamb and pumpkin is a delicious combination. Coco usually has two cakes per portion.

Makes: 4–5 portions

1 small onion, peeled
1 clove garlic, peeled and crushed
8oz/250g lean minced lamb
2 tablespoons fresh breadcrumbs (see page 123)
2oz/50g pumpkin mash (see page 21)
1 small egg, beaten
Butter or oil for frying

1 Put the onion and garlic in a food processor and chop. Add the mince, breadcrumbs and pumpkin mash and blend, adding the egg a little at a time. Form into 8 to 10 little cakes.

2 At this point you can either freeze the cakes or fry them. To freeze, place them flat on a tray lined with cling film. Cover the cakes with another layer of cling film and freeze. When frozen you can wrap them in pairs or individually. When needed, defrost the cakes in the fridge overnight.

3 Heat some butter or oil in a pan and fry over medium heat for 4 minutes on each side until cooked through.

pork schnitzel with lemon and thyme

I serve a "grown-up" version of this to Martin and the boys who love to eat the schnitzels with Fran's Fluffy Chips and Fresh Red Pepper and Tomato Salsa (see page 99). So does Coco, though her two schnitzels are a lot smaller!

Makes: 4 portions

8oz/225g pork fillet
2 teaspoons grated lemon zest
1 teaspoon fresh thyme
4 tablespoons dried breadcrumbs (see page 123)
Flour for coating
2 eggs, lightly beaten
Butter or oil for frying

1 Trim the fillet and cut into 8 ½in/1cm slices. Place each slice between two pieces of cling film and flatten with a rolling pin until quite thin.

2 Combine the lemon zest, thyme and breadcrumbs. Coat each slice of pork with flour, dip into the egg and then into the breadcrumb mixture.

3 At this point you can either freeze the schnitzels or fry them. To freeze, cover a tray with cling film and lay each slice on top. Cover again with film and freeze. When frozen, wrap into portions and put back into the freezer. When needed, defrost in the fridge overnight.

4 Heat some butter or oil in a pan and fry over medium heat for 2 to 3 minutes on each side until golden brown.

"lovely and lemony"

slow-braised duck legs with kumquats

The idea for this recipe came from the classic duck with orange. It is a very easy dish to prepare even if it sounds very grand – you just place all the ingredients in the oven and forget about it for the next hour and a half or so...

Makes: 6–8 portions

1 small onion, peeled
1 bay leaf
2 sprigs fresh thyme
1 clove garlic, peeled and crushed
2 duck legs (about 1½lb/750g)
3 kumquats, halved, or 1 orange, quartered
½ pint/275ml unsalted chicken stock (see page 125)
2 medium potatoes (about 8oz/225g), peeled and diced
1 small celeriac (about 8oz/225g), peeled and diced

1 Preheat the oven to 160ºC, 325ºF.

2 Put the onion in an ovenproof pan with the bay leaf, thyme and garlic. Place the duck legs and kumquat (or orange) on top and pour over the stock. Bring to the boil, cover and transfer to the oven. Cook for about 1 hour 40 minutes, or until the duck is tender.

3 Leave to cool. Then remove the herbs and strain over a bowl, reserving the cooking liquid.

4 Meanwhile, put the potatoes and celeriac in a saucepan and cover with cold water. Bring to the boil, cover and reduce the heat. Cook for about 20 minutes or until tender. Drain, mash and set aside.

5 Pick the duck meat from the bone and put into a food processor with one kumquat – don't put all of them in as they can be slightly bitter – and some of the onion. Roughly chop for older babies, or purée for younger ones.

6 Add the meat mixture to the celeriac and potato mash, adding more stock to correct the consistency if required. Divide into portions and serve or freeze.

more about...
kumquats

Orange-flavoured fruits similar in size to olives, kumquats have an edible rind and a slightly bitter taste.

cream cheese pastry sticks

Mum gave me this recipe – I haven't seen it before, but it is very similar to rough puff pastry. It is also great for sausage rolls or savoury turnovers. You can have fun trying out different shapes like hearts or triangles. Once you have brushed the pastry with egg, sprinkle it with poppy seeds, sesame seeds and – the boys' favourite – caraway seeds. Coco loves all of them!

These sticks cannot be frozen, but will keep in an airtight tin for up to two days. Serve them with the dips and spreads on pages 107 to 110.

Makes: 4–6 portions

4oz/100g plain flour
4oz/100g cream cheese
4oz/100g butter
Beaten egg for brushing

1 Preheat the oven to 230°C, 450°F.

2 Sift the flour into a mixing bowl, add the cheese and butter and mix together until it looks like coarse breadcrumbs. Bring the mix together into a ball, wrap with cling film and put it in the fridge overnight, or at least for a few hours, to become firm.

3 Roll out the pastry fairly thin, about ⅛in/3mm, brush with egg and cut into fingers.

4 Bake on a non-stick baking sheet for about 10 minutes until golden brown. Remove from the oven and allow to cool on the tray for about 5 minutes, then transfer to a cooling rack.

ham, leek and cheese pastry puffs

These make a lovely snack. If you plan to go shopping, take some with you to keep your little one happy (and quiet!).

Makes: 8 portions

Knob of unsalted butter
3 tablespoons/45ml water
1 leek (about 4–6oz/100–175g), finely
   sliced
2oz/50g hard cheese, grated
2oz/50g cooked ham, thinly sliced and
   finely diced
Flour for dusting
8oz/225g puff pastry
1 egg, beaten

1 Put the butter and water in a pan with the leek, cover with a tight-fitting lid and cook over medium heat for 8 to 10 minutes until tender. Leave to cool, then mix in the cheese and ham.

2 On a lightly floured surface, roll out the pastry to a thickness of about ⅛in/3mm. Then, using a 3¾in/10cm round cutter, cut out as many discs as you can (you should get about 8 to 10).

3 Place a heaped teaspoon of the leek, ham and cheese mixture in the centre of each disc of pastry. Brush the edges with the beaten egg, fold the discs in half and crimp well with your fingers or the tines of a fork dipped in flour to seal. Brush the puffs with the remaining beaten egg, place on a tray and freeze.

4 Cook from frozen for 20 to 25 minutes, until golden brown, in an oven preheated to 190ºC, 375ºF. When done, remove from the oven and allow to cool before serving.

preparation tip

If you are not going to freeze the puffs, leave them to rest in the fridge for at least 1 hour. Then bake for 10 minutes in an oven preheated to 200ºC, 400ºF.

pea and mint dip or spread

This is a fantastic combination – the freshness of the mint and the vibrant colour of the peas. You can use it as dip, or spread it on fresh crusty bread. Delicious! Coco usually uses her little finger to eat it.

Makes: 6 portions

8oz/225g defrosted peas
1 tablespoon chopped parsley
1 dessertspoon chopped mint
Juice of ½ lemon
1 teaspoon/5g sugar
4oz/100g cream cheese
1 small spring onion, chopped
Salt and pepper to taste (optional)

Simply put all the ingredients into a food processor and whiz! The dip is not suitable for freezing, but can be kept in the fridge in an airtight container for 2 days.

coco's tasty hummus

Tahini paste is made from pulped sesame seeds and gives the hummus its special flavour.

If you are in a hurry and haven't got time to soak the chick peas overnight, tinned ones are fine.

Makes: 6 portions

4oz/100g dried chick peas
1 clove garlic, peeled
Juice of ½ lemon
3 tablespoons/45ml good-quality olive oil
1 dessertspoon/10ml tahini paste
Pinch of cayenne pepper
Salt to taste (optional)

1 Soak the chick peas overnight. Rinse them and then put them in a saucepan, covering with fresh water. Bring to the boil and cook over medium heat, uncovered, for 1 to 1½ hours until tender. Strain over a bowl, reserving the cooking liquid.

2 Put all the ingredients into a food processor and whiz, adding some of the cooking liquid if required. The consistency should be like thick mayonnaise. The hummus is not suitable for freezing, but can be kept in the fridge in an airtight container for 2 days.

serving tip

We all love this dip served with breadsticks or raw vegetables, such as carrot or celery, or spread on toast.

tzatziki

I usually leave the dips and spreads overnight for the flavours to develop. I have to hide them from Martin though, because if he raids the fridge at night, they're usually gone by the morning!

If you have tzatziki left over, it can be kept in the fridge in an airtight container for up to 2 days.

Makes: 4 portions

1 cucumber, peeled
Salt for soaking
8oz/225g thick plain yoghurt
1 clove garlic, peeled and finely chopped
1 dessertspoon chopped dill
Pepper to taste (optional)

1 Cut the cucumber in half lengthwise and scrape out the seeds. Grate the cucumber into a non-reactive colander, sprinkle with salt and leave for about 45 minutes – this will get rid of a lot of the water in the cucumber.

2 Meanwhile, mix the yoghurt, garlic, dill and pepper in a bowl. Rinse the cucumber and squeeze it as dry as you can in a clean tea towel.

3 Add the cucumber to the yoghurt mix, stir and leave overnight in the fridge for the flavours to develop. This recipe is not suitable for freezing.

nutritional info

Cucumber is rich in folic acid, vitamin C and calcium. It has a high water content, making it refreshing and low in calories.

smoked salmon, chive & dill dip

Coco and I were on a shopping trip in Bath. It was cold and raining so I went to have a coffee to warm up and couldn't resist a freshly made smoked salmon and cream cheese sandwich. Coco was quite content with her banana until I started eating my sandwich, so I gave her some and all she said was "More, more!" as she picked out the salmon and cream cheese. So, I decided to try it at home and – surprise, surprise! – she loves it.

Makes: 4–6 portions

4oz/100g smoked salmon
14oz/400g cream cheese
1 dessertspoon chopped chives
1 dessertspoon chopped dill
Squeeze of fresh lemon juice

Put all the ingredients into a food processor and whiz. This dip is not suitable for freezing.

coco's guacamole dip

The classic guacamole has fresh chillies and lots of garlic, so it is very hot and spicy. I have toned down the recipe for Coco – she loves it with tortilla chips, which is great, as avocados are rich in nutrients.

Makes: 4–6 portions

2 ripe avocados, peeled and stoned
Squeeze of fresh lemon juice
2 dessertspoons/20ml crème frâiche
1 small clove garlic, peeled and
   chopped
1 small spring onion, chopped
1 tablespoon/15ml cold water
Salt and pepper to taste (optional)

Put all the ingredients into a food processor and whiz. The guacamole is not suitable for freezing, but can be kept in the fridge in an airtight container for 2 days, although it will start to discolour after a day.

creamy chicken liver spread

This is another really simple but delicious recipe. I made some at home over Christmas when friends came over for a drink. Coco, being Coco, helped herself – followed by a big "Ummm!"

Makes: 4 portions

6oz/175g unsalted butter
1oz/25g onion, peeled and chopped
1 small clove garlic, peeled and chopped
1oz/25g unsmoked bacon, diced
8oz/225g chicken livers, cleaned
2fl oz/55ml cold water
½ teaspoon sugar
Pinch of mace

1 Melt about 1oz/25g of the butter in a pan and fry the onion and garlic for 2 to 3 minutes.

2 Add the bacon and chicken livers and cook for a further 5 minutes, turning them over now and again until cooked. Add the water and stir the bottom of the pan to deglaze and mix in the juices. Pour the mix into a food processor.

3 Melt the rest of the butter in the same pan, then add to the chicken livers. Whiz to a smooth paste. The mixture might be a little grainy, so pass it through a sieve. This spread does not freeze well, but you can keep it in the fridge in an airtight container for 2 days.

serving tip

This makes a great canapé for adults too. When we served this in the restaurant, Martin used sherry or brandy in the mix, as well as a little cream, before stuffing it into choux pastry buns – delicious!

choux buns

I usually put a tray of water in the bottom of the oven to create steam to help the buns to rise. Choux buns will keep for one day, but they do freeze very well, too.

Makes: 18–20 buns

¼ pint/150ml water
2oz/50g unsalted butter
2½oz/60g plain flour
2 eggs, beaten
½ pint/300ml whipping cream
Icing sugar for dusting

1 Preheat the oven to 200°C, 400°F. Grease a baking tray and line with baking parchment or greaseproof paper.

2 Put the water and butter in a pan and bring to the boil. Turn off the heat and add the flour all at once, stirring vigorously with a wooden spoon until it is smooth.

3 Beat in the eggs a little at a time, mixing all the time until you have a firm, smooth, glossy paste.

4 Pipe the paste into little balls on the baking tray. Transfer to the oven and bake for about 25 to 30 minutes until crisp and rich golden in colour.

5 When cool, make a little hole in the bottom of each bun and pipe in some whipped cream. Dust with icing sugar and serve.

deep-fried rice pudding balls

This is one of Martin's creations and is very popular, not only with Coco, but also in the restaurant.

Makes: 6 portions

1 quantity rice pudding (see page 84)
1 quantity beer batter (see page 123)
Flour for coating
Caster sugar and cinnamon for dusting

1 Prepare the rice pudding and leave to cool, then put in the fridge to set.

2 Prepare the beer batter and leave to rest in the fridge.

3 When set, make the rice pudding into little balls, and roll them in flour. Dip them into the batter and deep-fry (180°C/350°F) until golden brown. Dust with sugar and cinnamon.

4 Serve with raspberry sauce (see page 88) or with one of the mango purées (see pages 71 and 87).

basic scones

This is also the dough I use to make my Quick Pizza (see page 30).

Makes: 10–12 scones (or 8oz/225g dough for pizza)

1–2oz/25–50g unsalted butter
8oz/225g self-raising flour
¼ pint/150ml milk

1 Preheat the oven to 220ºC, 425ºF.

2 Rub the butter into the flour until the mixture resembles coarse breadcrumbs.

3 Make a well in the centre and mix with enough milk to make a soft dough. (Now it is ready to be used for quick pizza.)

4 Roll the dough to a thickness of ¾in/2cm and cut into rounds. Put on a greased baking tray, brush the top with a little milk and bake near the top of the oven for about 10 minutes. Leave to cool, cut in half and serve with butter.

sweet potato scones

A lovely variation on an old favourite. The dough is very soft, so handle with care. Neither of the scone recipes are suitable for freezing.

Makes: 10–12 scones

6oz/175g sweet potatoes, peeled and cut into small chunks
8oz/225g plain flour
2oz/50g light brown sugar
1 tablespoon baking powder
½ teaspoon ground mace
2oz/50g butter
2 teaspoons chopped chives
2fl oz/55ml milk

1 Put the sweet potatoes in a saucepan. Cover with cold water, bring to the boil, cover and boil for 5 to 10 minutes until tender. Then drain, mash and leave to cool.

2 Preheat the oven to 220ºC, 425ºF.

3 Put all the dry ingredients into a bowl and rub the butter into it until it resembles breadcrumbs. Add the sweet potato, chives and milk.

4 Roll out to a thickness of ¾in/2cm and cut into rounds. Put on a greased baking tray and bake for 10 to 12 minutes. Leave to cool and serve.

variations

Fruit scones
Add about 2oz/50g of any dried fruit to the basic scone mix at the end of step 2.

Savoury scones
Add 2–3oz/50–75g grated Cheddar cheese to the basic scone mix at the end of step 2.

flap jacks

These are very sweet but make a nice treat, and the oats are extremely nutritious. They don't freeze well.

Makes: 12 squares

1oz/25g demerara sugar
4oz/100g unsalted butter
2 tablespoons/10ml golden syrup
8oz/225g rolled oats
Pinch salt

1 Preheat the oven to 190ºC, 375ºF. Grease a baking tin of about 10in/25cm x 8in/20cm and line with baking parchment or greaseproof paper.

2 Melt the sugar, butter and syrup together in a bowl in a saucepan or in the microwave. Add the oats and mix well. Put the mixture into the tin and bake for 30 to 40 minutes until brown.

3 Remove from the oven and when set (after about 10 minutes), cut into pieces but leave in the tin until cold.

rock cakes

The boys love these when they come home from school, and whatever the boys love, so does Coco. Max says it makes the house smell cosy! You can keep the rock cakes in an airtight container for up to 2 days, but they don't freeze well.

Makes: 10–12 cakes

4oz/100g unsalted butter
8oz/225g self-raising flour
Pinch of salt
¼ teaspoon ground mixed spice
4oz/100g caster sugar
4oz/100g currants or sultanas
1 egg, lightly beaten
Milk to mix

1 Preheat the oven to 200ºC, 400ºF. Grease a baking tray and line with baking parchment or greaseproof paper.

2 Rub the butter into the flour until it resembles fine breadcrumbs. Stir in the other dry ingredients, as well as the currants or sultanas, and make a well in the centre. Pour in the egg and a little milk and mix to a stiff dough – you might need to add a little more milk.

3 Spoon the mixture into small piles on the baking tray. Bake for about 15 to 20 minutes, until just firm to the touch.

coco's favourite brownies (and leon's and max's)

Mum used to cook these for me and my two brothers, Huw and Richard, when we were little. You can't beat the smell – even our crazy Siamese cat used to sit right by the oven door when Mum baked them. I don't have a cat now, but I have three children who do the same. As soon as the brownies are cold enough to eat, they're gone!

The better quality of dark chocolate you use, the better the end result. Try serving the brownies warm with ice-cream or custard.

Makes: 12 squares

3½oz/100g butter
6oz/175g caster sugar
½ teaspoon vanilla essence or arôme
1oz/25g drinking chocolate
2 eggs, beaten
2oz/50g dark chocolate, melted
4oz/100g walnuts, chopped (optional)
3oz/75g plain flour
½ teaspoon baking powder

1 Preheat the oven to 190ºC, 375ºF. Grease an 8in/20cm square tin and line it with baking parchment or greaseproof paper.

2 Cream the butter and sugar together until light and fluffy. Slowly beat in the vanilla, drinking chocolate and eggs, then the melted chocolate. Stir in the nuts (if using) and mix well, then add the flour and baking powder.

3 Spread the mixture into the tin and bake for 30 to 35 minutes until the sponge is cooked. Cut into squares and leave to cool. The brownies cannot be frozen, but can be kept in an airtight container for up to 2 days.

"can I have another?"

coconut and chocolate chip cookies

These home-made cookies taste far better than the shop-bought ones – but you need to be ready to make another batch as they go very quickly, and it isn't Coco who eats them all!

Makes: 20–24 cookies

4oz/100g unsalted butter
4oz/100g dark brown sugar
2oz/50g caster sugar
Few drops vanilla essence or arôme
1 egg, beaten
½ teaspoon bicarbonate of soda
7oz/200g plain flour, sieved
4oz/100g chocolate chips
2oz/50g desiccated coconut

1 Preheat the oven to 180ºC, 350ºF. Line a large baking tray with baking parchment or greaseproof paper.

2 Cream the butter and sugars together until light and fluffy. Add the vanilla and egg a little at a time, stirring constantly. Then add the bicarbonate of soda, flour, chocolate chips and coconut and combine all together with a large spoon.

3 Place heaped teaspoons of the mix on the baking tray, about 2in/5cm apart. Bake for 10 to 15 minutes until lightly coloured. These will keep in an airtight tin for 2 to 3 days, but they don't freeze well.

"where are
my cookies?"

orange biscuits

These biscuits are very sweet when made with icing in the middle. I prefer them as dry biscuits but, of course, the children love the butter icing.

Try to buy unwaxed oranges, but if you can't, wash the orange to remove any wax before zesting it and take care not to include any of the white pith, as it is bitter.

Makes: 20 biscuits

For the biscuits:
4oz/100g caster sugar
4oz/100g butter
Grated zest of 1 orange
1 dessertspoon/10ml golden syrup
1 egg yolk
7oz/200g plain flour
1 teaspoon/5g baking powder

For the icing:
3oz/75g icing sugar
A little orange zest
2 teaspoons/10ml orange juice
1½oz/40g butter

To make the biscuits

1 Preheat the oven to 190ºC, 375ºF. Grease a baking tray and line with baking parchment or greaseproof paper.

2 Cream the sugar, butter and orange zest together. Add the golden syrup and egg yolk and then mix in the flour and baking powder.

3 Form the mixture into small balls (the mix is quite crumbly). Place the balls well apart on the baking tray and press lightly. Bake for 20 to 25 minutes until golden. The biscuits will spread slightly and crinkle like macaroons.

4 Remove from the oven and allow to cool on the tray for about 5 minutes before transferring to a cooling rack. These will keep in an airtight tin for 2 to 3 days, but they don't freeze well.

To make the orange butter icing

5 Sift the icing sugar into a bowl. Cream together with the zest, juice and butter.

6 Use the icing to sandwich the orange biscuits together.

lemon curd

This is so easy to make and has a fantastic fresh flavour. When Coco tried it for the first time she winced. I then gave it to her on toast and she really took to it.

Try to get unwaxed lemons, but if you can't, make sure you wash them to remove the wax.

Makes: about 8fl oz/225ml

2 lemons
2 eggs
2oz/50g butter
4oz/100g sugar

1 Finely grate the zest from the lemons, making sure you don't include any of the white pith, as it is very bitter, then squeeze out the juice. Put the zest and juice into a large bowl with the eggs, butter and sugar.

2 Place over a pan of hot water and cook over medium heat, whisking all the time. When the curd starts to thicken, reduce the heat and keep whisking until it loses its translucency. Remove from the heat, but keep whisking off the heat for a few minutes for a lighter, fluffy curd. This takes about 15 to 20 minutes in total.

3 When finished, leave to cool. This will keep sealed in a jar in the fridge for up to 2 weeks, but cannot be frozen.

variation

For a simple pudding, mix two parts crème frâiche to one part lemon curd and serve as it is or freeze for a lovely zesty ice cream – it will set very hard, so remove from the freezer about 10 minutes before you need it.

exotic fruit salad

This makes a refreshing change from a usual fruit salad. Coco loves it and it freezes really well too! Make sure the fruit is really ripe.

Lychees, originally from China, have a lovely sweet, perfumed flavour similar to elderflowers. They contain good amounts of vitamin C.

Makes: 4–6 portions

½ small pineapple, peeled and cored
1 large kiwi fruit, peeled
4 lychees, peeled and stoned
½ paw-paw, peeled and seeds removed
½ mango, peeled and stone removed
4 large strawberries, hulled
Juice of 1 large orange

Cut all the fruit into small dice, mix and add the orange juice. Leave in the fridge for an hour for all the flavours to develop. Lovely served on its own or with ice-cream.

apricot, date and walnut chews

This is another of Mum's old-fashioned baking recipes. Dad was the one who used to finish these before they were cool – he loved dates! If you don't want to use nuts, just add another dried fruit such as pears, prunes or sultanas. Full of natural flavour and, unlike shop-bought chews, not packed with preservatives and loads of sugar.

Makes: 12 chews

6oz/175g dried apricots
6oz/175g dates
4oz/100g walnuts
1oz/25g butter, melted
1 dessertspoon light brown sugar
1 tablespoon/10g self-raising flour
1 egg
Caster sugar for dusting

1 Preheat the oven to 190ºC, 375ºF. Grease an 8in/20cm square sandwich tin and line with baking parchment or greaseproof paper.

2 Put the apricots, dates and walnuts into a food processor and finely chop. Put into a bowl with the butter, sugar, flour and egg and mix thoroughly. Press into the tin.

3 Bake for about 35 minutes. When cold, cut into small squares and dust with caster sugar. These will keep in an airtight tin for up to 3 days – if they last that long! They don't freeze well.

basic recipes

On the following pages you will find recipes that are used throughout the book in different dishes. For easy reference, I have put them in one chapter.

I have also included recipes for basic stocks if you want to make your own. Of course you don't have to if you don't have the time – there are some good low-salt ones available from health food shops and some supermarkets. (Always read the nutritional information to double check.)

Many supermarkets also make their own fresh stock (usually found near the meat counters). These taste good, can be low in salt and free of additives, but they usually work out to be expensive. So, if you can, make your own and freeze it in batches.

potato mash

basic white sauce

Easy to make, potato mash is used in a great many recipes in this book as it blends well with most vegetables.

Makes: 12oz/350g mash

3 medium potatoes (about 12oz/350g)

1 Peel and dice the potatoes and put in a saucepan. Cover with cold water and bring to the boil. Cover, reduce the heat and cook for about 20 minutes or until tender.

2 Drain the potatoes and mash with a fork, masher or potato ricer. Do not use a food processor to mash the potatoes, as this will make them go gluey.

This is a fantastic way to make a white sauce without the fuss of making a roux first – great when you are pushed for time.

For babies under 12 months, use baby's usual formula to make the sauce and check with your health visitor before changing from formula to cow's milk.

Makes: 1 pint/570ml

1 pint/570ml cold milk
2oz/50g butter
1½oz/40g plain flour
1 bay leaf

1 Simply put all the ingredients into a heavy-bottomed pan. The milk must be cold or you will get a lumpy sauce.

2 Place the pan over medium heat, whisking all the time until the sauce starts to thicken. Reduce the heat and simmer gently for about 5 minutes, stirring occasionally. Remove the bay leaf before using.

variations

Cheese sauce
Add about 2oz/50g grated hard cheese to the hot white sauce, whisking until the cheese has melted.

Velouté
Instead of milk, use stock to make this sauce (see page 58).

Dill sauce for poached salmon
After poaching salmon, remove the fish and reserve the milk. Make the white sauce using the poaching milk, and add some chopped dill at the end.

fresh tomato sauce

Tinned tomatoes are great to keep in the cupboard and to use when you're in a hurry, but they do contain a little bit of salt. If you want your baby's food to be completely salt-free, it's easy enough to make your own fresh tomato sauce to use in the recipes.

Makes: 14oz/400g

1 tablespoon/15ml olive oil
1 small onion, chopped
2lb/900g fresh, ripe tomatoes,
    skinned, seeded and chopped
    (about 14oz/400g after skinning and
    seeding)

1 Heat the oil in a pan over medium heat. Add the onion and gently fry for about 5 minutes until soft.

2 Add the tomatoes and bring to a simmer. Reduce the heat and cook, uncovered, for about 10 minutes or until the tomatoes are tender.

3 Use in the recipe straight away or keep in the fridge for 2 days. You can also freeze the tomato sauce in batches for later use; it will be easier to use if you defrost it first.

beer batter

This batter is lovely and light and really quick. Use it for Deep-fried Rice Pudding Balls (see page 111), or for frying small pieces of fish or chicken. This makes a fair amount of batter, so it is worth frying for the whole family as it does not keep well.

Don't worry about giving your baby beer – all the alcohol evaporates in the frying – but you can use sparkling mineral water instead of beer.

Makes: ½ pint/275ml

1 sachet (1 slightly heaped teaspoon/7g), fast-acting bread yeast
9fl oz/250ml beer (lager)
Pinch salt
Pinch sugar
1 teaspoon/5ml white wine vinegar
6½oz/180g plain flour

1 In a large mixing bowl, dissolve the yeast in the beer, then add the salt, sugar and vinegar.

2 Sieve the flour over the liquid and beat until smooth and creamy. You may need to add more liquid if the batter is too thick.

3 Place in the fridge for about 20 minutes before use.

4 Dip rice balls or fish or chicken pieces in the batter and deep-fry (180°C/350°F) until golden brown.

breadcrumbs

Don't be tempted to use pre-sliced factory loaves for crumbs. These loaves contain so many additives to give them a long shelf life that the results will be less than satisfactory.

Fresh
For fresh breadcrumbs use a good white loaf. Cut off the crusts (keep these for dried breadcrumbs). Roughly cut up or tear the bread, put in a food processor and work until broken down into soft crumbs. I use these fresh crumbs for binding meatballs.

Dried
Collect left-over bread and crusts. Spread out on a baking tray and place in a warm, just turned-off oven. (Great to do if you have just finished the Sunday roast; saves energy, too). When the bread has gone hard and cold, pop it into a processor and work until fine. You can keep the crumbs in an airtight container for about 2 weeks. I use them for crumbing my Fish Cakes and Goujons (see pages 93 to 95).

stock recipes

brown beef stock

Makes: 4 pints/2.25 litres

2lb/900g beef bones (such as rib bones), chopped into evenly sized pieces
1 onion (about 4oz/100g), quartered
1 carrot (about 4oz/100g), cut into ½in/15mm lengths
1 leek (about 4oz/100g), halved
2 stalks celery (about 4oz/100g), halved
4 pints/2.25 litres water
6 tomatoes, halved and seeds scooped out
Small bunch parsley
1 sprig thyme
4 black peppercorns
1 bay leaf

1 Preheat the oven to 230ºC, 450ºF. Place the bones and all the vegetables, except the tomatoes, in a roasting tin and roast in the oven for 20 to 30 minutes until browned, turning the bones and vegetables now and again. The vegetables are kept in quite large pieces, so that they won't burn while roasting.

2 Drain off any fat and transfer the bones and vegetables to a large saucepan. Deglaze the roasting tin by swilling with a little boiling water and simmering for a few minutes on the hob.

3 Add the juices to the saucepan with the bones and vegetables. Add the water, tomatoes, herbs and seasonings, bring to the boil and skim. Simmer for approximately 2 to 2½ hours, skimming now and again. Strain and cool. Remove any fat from the top before using or freezing in batches.

chicken stock

Makes: 3 pints/1.75 litres

1 onion (about 4oz/100g)
1 carrot (about 4oz/100g)
1 leek (about 4oz/100g)
1 stalk celery (about 2oz/50g)
2lb/900g chicken bones, chopped
3 pints/1.75 litres water
Small bunch parsley
1 sprig thyme
4 black peppercorns
1 bay leaf

Wash and chop all the vegetables into evenly sized pieces. Place all the ingredients into a saucepan, bring to the boil and skim. Simmer gently for about 1 hour without a lid, skimming now and again. Strain, cool and remove any fat from the top before using or freezing in batches.

fish stock

Makes: 1 pint/570ml

½ onion (about 2oz/50g), peeled and sliced
1 carrot (about 4oz/100g), peeled and diced
1lb/450g fish bones, chopped
1 pint/570ml water
Juice of ½ lemon
Few stalks parsley
3 black peppercorns
1 bay leaf

Put all the ingredients in a large saucepan. Bring to simmering point and simmer, uncovered, for about 20 minutes. Remove from the heat and strain over a bowl. Use or freeze in batches.

white vegetable stock

Makes: 3 pints/1.75 litres

1 large onion (about 5oz/150g)
1 large carrot (about 5oz/150g)
1 large leek (about 5oz/150g)
2–3 stalks celery (about 5oz/150g)
1 courgette (about 5oz/150g)
3 pints/1.75 litres water
1 clove garlic, peeled and chopped
Small bunch parsley
1 sprig thyme
4 black peppercorns
1 bay leaf

Wash and chop all the vegetables into evenly sized pieces. Place all the ingredients into a saucepan, bring to the boil and skim if necessary. Simmer for 40 minutes, allow to cool and strain over a bowl. Use or freeze in batches.

index

acknowledgements

Carroll and Brown would like to thank:
Karol Davies, Nigel Reed and Paul Stradling for production
Hilary Bird for the index

Siân would like to thank:
Bina – for her tireless help and support in typing all the recipes and making sense of all my scribbles. A big thank you, I couldn't have done it without her. Also Mike for his IT support!
Martin – for putting up with my constant talk of baby foods, for his culinary tips, never-ending patience and support
Andy – for all his fantastic photographs of Coco; they speak for themselves
Leon, Max and Coco – my professional little tasters
Rosemary – who believed in me enough to take this forward
Helen of Bath Catering College – for her help with nutritional values
Jekka – for her knowledge of herbs
Jan – my health visitor
Julie and Patrick – for their love and support, especially over this last year
Jo and her mum, Jenny – for their help with Coco
Izzy – for being Coco's best friend and fellow taster
Also Penny, Mitch, Tom, Ali, Rosie, Fran, and Callum

"It is amazing how different people from different walks of life all come to the same conclusion at the same time. In this case, Siân and I independently came to the conclusion that something had to be done about the state of the baby food market.

Commercially available baby food is old hat and needed modernising since it was all khaki in colour and regardless of what was in it, it all tasted the same. What I have done is brought what's on offer up to date by developing commercially available frozen baby food. At the same time Siân decided to write a book to encourage parents that it is not difficult to make good-quality, nutritious baby food at home and then freeze it for another day!

Babylicious is there for the days when you are a bit too busy to get out the blenders and is in total harmony with everything in Cooking for Coco. I am delighted to be working with Siân from a different angle to help raise the standard of the food fed to babies. Why do we treat baby food as a cheap commodity?

Siân has shown it can be fun and easy to make your own baby food that is appetising and nutritious, and we wish her book every success in encouraging young mothers to have a go!"

Sally Preston, Founder and Managing Director, Babylicious Ltd